To. Cherie
Best Wishes
Thank you—

6/17/23

Remember Their Sacrifice

Remember Their Sacrifice

Stories of Unheralded Athletes of Color

Arif Khatib
Pete Elman

ROWMAN & LITTLEFIELD
Lanham • Boulder • New York • London

Published by Rowman & Littlefield
An imprint of The Rowman & Littlefield Publishing Group, Inc.
4501 Forbes Boulevard, Suite 200, Lanham, Maryland 20706
www.rowman.com

86-90 Paul Street, London EC2A 4NE, United Kingdom

British Library Cataloguing in Publication Information Available

Library of Congress Cataloging-in-Publication Data Available

ISBN 9781538171974 (cloth) | ISBN 9781538171981 (ebook)

This book is dedicated to the many athletes of color who paved the way for countless others who never received proper recognition; for those whose historic contributions would someday benefit sports and society. Despite the tremendous obstacles in their path, these courageous athletes persevered and left important legacies.

Contents

Foreword

Dave Zirin

As a history major in college, I came to savor the way our past can inform our present and future. I treasured the quote from Malcolm X that was on a poster tacked to the wall of my dormitory: "Of all our studies, history is best qualified to reward our research. And when you see that you've got problems, all you have to do is examine the historic method used all over the world by others who have problems similar to yours. And once you see how they got theirs straight, then you know how you can get yours straight."

That is absolutely true. But what do you do when you have a generation of young people who either are not taught history or find it presented to them in a way so monotonous it could make an overcaffeinated teenager drowsy with boredom? When that happens, we must find new ways to present the past in a far more dynamic fashion. This is vital not just to teach in the present but because the future depends on it.

When I was teaching a class titled Sports History in the United States at Montgomery College in Maryland, I had students whose knowledge of American history was neither wide nor deep. They were largely taking the class because it fulfilled a requirement, not out of a love for the topic. These were extremely intelligent students who simply had never been taught about the rambling highs and low points of the remarkable roller coaster that has been the history of the United States. What I learned, however, from teaching the class was that these students could be reached by using sports to tell the broader narrative of this country. I learned that the games we play could be a pedagogical Trojan horse, taking a subject many of them had written off as a musty, pointless exercise in learning dates and making it come alive.

I came to appreciate, and I believe my students grew to understand, that sports is a remarkable lens through which to learn about the history of the United States. If you want to understand the overcoming of Jim Crow segregation, the odyssey of Jackie Robinson tells that story with remarkable and crackling clarity. If you want to explore the women's movement, the push for equity by Billie Jean King and her epic Battle of the Sexes match against Bobby Riggs makes it plain. If you want to better comprehend the 1960s and how the United States eventually turned against the war in Vietnam, look no further than Muhammad Ali and the way he went from the most despised athlete in the United States, his very heavyweight title stripped from his waist, to someone with a massive amen chorus in just a few years.

These are some of the most famous sports narratives. They opened my students' minds. Yet they are also the ones that many of us already know and hold close to our hearts. Beyond the lionized sports heroes, there is also a treasure trove of other tales in sports history, ones that tell equally powerful narratives both poignant and pugnacious. In many respects, these stories are more valuable because they move us beyond idols and heroes to the ways that ordinary people took extraordinary steps to use sports as a platform for advancement, resistance, and even protest. Now we have a book to introduce a new generation of readers to those we should count among the true change makers in sports history, yet whose stories have for too long been ignored.

Remember Their Sacrifice: Stories of Unheralded Athletes of Color, by Arif Khatib and Pete Elman, brings to life many whose triumphs have for too long been buried. These are the trailblazers, and they deserve to be not only treasured but examined so that we can learn the lessons of their mighty accomplishments and their triumphs over not only opponents on the field of play but also over an unequal society set up to hold them back.

If you want to know about the history of racism in Boston, a city with a tradition both proudly liberal and brutally prejudiced, learn the story of Elijah "Pumpsie" Green, told eloquently here. Pumpsie Green was the first Black player to take the field for the storied Boston Red Sox as they became the last team to integrate, all the way up to 1959, twelve years after Jackie Robinson took the field for the Brooklyn Dodgers.

People may know the story of *A League of Their Own*, the 1992 film about the All-American Girls Professional Baseball League. But if you want to really learn about the experience of women and baseball, you need to know about Toni Stone, one of three women who played in the Negro Leagues in the 1950s. The story of Toni Stone getting a single off legendary pitcher Satchel Paige should be one that every sports fan knows. Instead, it has been lost to time. Khatib and Elman don't only revive it; they make the moment come alive.

The timing of this book could not be better. We are living in a moment when a new generation of athletes is learning how to use their hyper-exalted platform to speak out about the inequities of our world. In the years since Colin Kaepernick first took a knee during the national anthem to protest police violence, we have seen hundreds of high school, college, and professional athletes take that tentative step toward being more than just jocks and refusing to just "shut up and play." A book like this will give confidence to those who aren't LeBron James: people in small towns playing their sports on hardscrabble fields in front of a few dozen fans. It will give them confidence that they are part of a proud tradition of athletes who refused to bow down. Their resilience is the backbone of this book, and it's the backbone of a tradition that with electric clarity has come alive to light the way in a time of wretched darkness.

Acknowledgments

We would like to thank our many friends in the fields of journalism and education for their encouragement and support in assembling this project. Special thanks to Dr. Bob Allen, Doug Harris, Urla Hill, Arne Lang, John Lutz, Mike McGreehan, and Rikki Stevenson. Shout-outs to legendary Bay Area sportswriter Dave Newhouse for his assistance; Christopher Weills of the *Ultimate Sports Guide* for his encouragement; and the progressive voice of American sports, Dave Zirin of *The Nation* magazine, for his contribution of the foreword.

About the Book

This book tells the story of the journey, struggles, and achievements of a special group of unheralded athletes of color. In these pages you will learn about a handful of brave trailblazers, men and women whose skills and exploits contributed to an array of individual and team sports such as track and field, golf, diving, basketball, football, baseball, and martial arts. We must elevate these pioneers to their deserved position in the pantheon of sports. Our goal here is to educate, to shed light on a group of unsung individuals who by their example have inspired us.

Introduction

The history of America has been written by men and women of every color and ethnicity. Athletes of color have stood tall during both disappointments and triumphs, and throughout history they have displayed tremendous courage both on and off the field. This has been accomplished by determination and by rising above segregation and stereotypes to become leaders in every facet of American life.

These athletes only began to participate in the Olympics in 1904. Once they were finally able to compete, they were eventually able to succeed in and even dominate many sports. The color lines fell slowly but surely. Their achievements in sports in general and the Olympics in particular are historic and extraordinary. These men and women were sustained by a culture of unity, purpose, and faith. They knew the eyes of the world were focused on them and that they had to excel to push doors open for others.

The first African American to participate in the Olympics was George Poage in 1904 in St. Louis, where he won two bronze medals in the 200 meters and 400 meters. The first Black to earn a gold medal in the Olympics was John Baxter Taylor, who won gold with the 1,600-meter relay team in 1908 in London. He won a spot on the team after he graduated from the University of Pennsylvania School of Veterinary Medicine. The second was Joseph Stadler, who won a silver medal in the high jump and a bronze medal in the triple jump the same year.

Sports have the power to change the world. In 1934 the Italian dictator Benito Mussolini used the World Cup to further fascism. And that was one of Adolf Hitler's intentions for the 1936 Olympics in Berlin, to prove the superiority of the Aryan race through sport. That myth was exploded when African American runners Jesse

Owens, Archie Williams, and John Woodruff stunned the world by winning six gold medals, setting world records in Berlin.

Woodruff caused the Berlin crowd to gasp when he came to a complete stop while running and winning the 800 meters. The August 4, 1936, issue of the *New York Herald Tribune* called it "the most daring move ever seen on a track."

John Woodruff was among the thirteen Olympians inducted into the African American Ethnic Sports Hall of Fame at the 2004 Olympic trials in Sacramento, California, along with Poage, Edith McGuire-Duvall, John Carlos, Tommie Smith, Wyomia Tyus, Lee Evans, Harrison Dillard, Reginald Pearman, Herbert Douglas, Wilbur Ross, Milt Campbell, and Alice Coachman.

Each athlete who was inducted that day exemplified the attributes of loyalty and respect for the rules of fair play and dedication to America. And they were moving like a European train—fast and on time. The theme for that ceremony was coined by gold medalist Olympic runner Mal Whitfield, who said that day, "From the Auction Blocks . . . to the Olympic Starting Blocks."

At those trials, the African American Ethnic Sports Hall of Fame celebrated one hundred years of African American participation in the Olympics, and not surprisingly there were no parades or other celebrations in communities of color. During the ceremony, it was said, "Never before and probably never again," a historical reference to the fact that the inducted athletes, both dead and living, had never been honored in the same room, and probably never would be again.

That sentiment was expressed by Willye White. White, a five-time Olympian sprinter, participated in the celebration of those thirteen Black Olympians, their careers spanning from 1904 to 1968. The event was entered into the Congressional Record of the House of Representatives when thirteen-term California congresswoman, the Honorable Barbara Lee, rose to honor the induction of these Olympians.

In 2007, longtime Bay Area sportswriter Dave Newhouse wrote a beautiful piece in the *East Bay Times* about the Tuskegee Airmen, in which he described those World War II heroes as "once disgraced . . . now embraced," a phrase that could be applied to these athletes as well. The treatment of Blacks in America is directly connected to the transatlantic slave trade. Blacks struggled and continue to struggle against a system of oppression. They were forced to hold on to each other and help build a nation that didn't want them. They knew that American society was based on systemic racism, and they were prepared to face a plethora of challenges. Systemic racism is when in-place systems and policies create inequality and restrictions on an entire group of people.

From the beginning in this country, African Americans have been segregated and denied access to adequate food, shelter, and opportunities for education. But they have shown incredible resilience despite the many obstacles placed in their path.

African American athletes realized that sports could be a vehicle to break down barriers and foster greater understanding. Some of our most effective goodwill ambassadors have come from our athletic ranks.

Much of the source material for this book comes from interviews and articles that appeared in the *African American Sports Magazine*, which was published by the African American Ethnic Sports Hall of Fame, as well as induction ceremony transcripts. The African American Ethnic Hall of Fame was established by Arif Khatib in 2000 to bring attention to the treatment of minority athletes in the sports world by inducting those who were overlooked by other sports halls of fame. Since then, over 300 athletes and coaches and 275 community leaders have been enshrined in or honored by the African American Ethnic Hall of Fame.

These individuals followed a road paved with the land mines of injustice, racism, bigotry, and discrimination. In 2009, as society became more inclusive to multiracial, multicultural, and multiethnic people, Khatib chose to induct not just athletes of color into the hall of fame. He felt it was time to induct nonminority athletes who have made significant contributions to their chosen sports and their communities; thus was born the Multi-Ethnic Sports Hall of Fame, the name by which it has been known from 2009 to the present. Throughout the book we have used the hall of fame's original name, however, since that is what it was called when these individuals were inducted.

When the request was made for nonminorities to be nominated, the hall of fame received well over fifty names. "I think adjusting this hall of fame to include all humans, regardless of color, is a brilliant stroke," said Monte Poole, longtime respected sports columnist and current Comcast Sports analyst. "Some might believe any change would dilute the hall of fame, make it somehow less pure. The way I see it, you'd be recognizing not just the color of one's skin but all those, regardless of skin color, who contributed to the cause of equality." Khatib, the founder, relinquished his presidency in 2018 but continues to serve as president emeritus.

Athletes of color also made history when Maritza Correia became the first Puerto Rican of African descent to be a member of the U.S. Olympic swimming team in 2004. In the 2005 issue of *African American Sports Magazine*, Correia said, "I can't tell you how good this feels, just to have made the team."

And when track star Ana Guevara crossed the finish line in Paris after running the fastest quarter mile of her life, she became the first Mexican runner to win the 400-meter run at the World Track and Field Championship or the Olympics. "My country will be very happy. Now I'm compared with all the other people of sports, the boxing, baseball and football people. This victory changed a lot of minds," said Guevara in the 2008 issue of *African American Sports Magazine.*

When asked once again to support the nomination of the late Curt Flood, whose story is told in these pages, to the Baseball Hall of Fame, Khatib held fast to the belief that Flood was a person who changed the face of sports with his brave stand in 1971, when he took his case arguing against baseball's reserve clause all the way to the Supreme Court. Although Flood lost, his action led the way to free agency, and his sacrifice created opportunities for hundreds of other athletes who today are receiving astronomical contracts.

It is a travesty that Curt Flood is not in the Baseball Hall of Fame. His terrific career combined with the fearless courage he displayed in the face of great opposition should have guaranteed him a spot long ago. "I enthusiastically sign the annual petition from his daughter for his nomination, and the fact he has been bypassed each year has helped provide the inspiration and impetus for this book," said Khatib.

Khatib was a friend of Flood's, and he promised Curt that he would keep his story before the public. There is a proposal in front of the City of Oakland to present an annual event in which the Curt Flood Platinum Award will be presented to the most valuable player from each major sport that benefited from Curt's effort to create free agency. The event will not only shine a light on Flood's deserving of hall of fame status but also bring visibility to Curt Flood Field in Oakland, a neglected youth ball field that, if renovated, can be a beacon for young ballplayers.

There are hundreds of world-class athletes of color who have never been properly recognized, like Billy Mills, a Native American and winner of the gold medal in the 10,000-meter run at the 1964 Tokyo Olympics, whose story appears in this book. A member of the Lakota Sioux tribe, he is also featured in the documentary film *Because They Believed.* Mills is a track legend, but not a lot of people are aware of his compelling story.

Mills was the first non-European to win the Olympic 10,000 meters. No American has won that event since. In describing a conversation they shared, Khatib said, "Since we were friends, he shared something with me he had not shared before. And his story is riveting. It will bring tears to your eyes when he recalls his youth on the Sioux reservation."

The Negro baseball leagues flourished during the first half of the twentieth century and contributed tremendously to American baseball history. The perseverance demonstrated by these men who simply wanted to "play ball" is an untold story that's finally being told. But in these pages you will learn the stories of two brave women, Mamie "Peanut" Johnson and Toni Stone, who played in the Negro Leagues in the 1950s. That era offered a fascinating glimpse into American sports and revealed a rich and colorful story that had a profound impact on not only our national pastime but also America's social and moral development in the twentieth century.

Throughout history, marginalized people have displayed great courage and skill in music, art, literature, dance, film, politics, and other endeavors. In sports, there are constant reminders of the struggles, trials, and tribulations that athletes of color have endured; hopefully others will better understand the shoulders we all stand on.

When minorities were finally allowed to participate in the Olympics and other sports, they succeeded. This was accomplished by determination and rising above segregation and stereotypes. They played a pivotal role in the shaping of sports in America. These athletes were committed to leaving the world better than they found it; they were trailblazers who defied the odds, broke down barriers, and raised the bar of excellence.

Their accomplishments bring hope to young people that children of color no longer have to endure the indignities of yesteryear. Today these children grow up knowing they can achieve greatness because of the athletes before them. The history of America has been written by men and women of every color and ethnicity who have stood tall during disappointments as well as the good times. So we are humbled and give respect to athletes of color who sacrificed their careers for the cause of social justice. Discrimination continues, but the attempt to prevent athletes of color from achieving their goals will fail.

An example from our history reveals the character of courage. Despite the abolition of slavery in the state of New York in 1827, New York City remained segregated. In 1854, Elizabeth Jennings, a schoolteacher, became the first to challenge segregation on the subway when she was told she must board the car only with other Black people. In a November 13, 2005, article in the *New York Times*, "The Schoolteacher and the Streetcar," Katherine Greider described what Jennings said that day: "I told the conductor I was a respectable person, born and raised in New York . . . and that he was a good-for-nothing impudent fellow for insulting a decent person."

Lucy Foster was the first Black student to enroll at the University of Alabama. Just a week before her death, Foster spoke at a ceremony for a campus building being dedicated in her name at the college. The Associated Press quoted her in a March 2, 2022, article as saying, "If I am a master teacher, what I hope I am teaching you is that love will take care of everything in our world, don't you think? It's not your color. It's not how bright you are. It is how you feel about those that you deal with."

Let us be mindful that a truly free nation cannot be so long as one person suffers from discrimination. Collectively, we can make a difference in how history is told. Our young people can and will excel if given the opportunity, encouragement, and support they need. This book describes the trials, tribulations, and triumphs of brave and talented athletes. We hope that you enjoy it and are able to gain some insight and derive inspiration from their heartfelt stories.

1

A Trailblazer Has No Regrets

Pumpsie Green

Fenway Park, August 4, 1959: The Boston Red Sox are playing a doubleheader against the Kansas City Athletics. Striding nervously to the plate in the first game to lead off the bottom of the first inning, wearing number 12, is a twenty-five-year-old rookie second baseman from California who has patiently worked his way up through the minor leagues and is now finally in "the show."

Brought up to the parent club in July after hitting a torrid .320 for the Red Sox triple-A affiliate Minneapolis Millers, he has already appeared in eight games on the road, hitting at a .300 clip while flashing a sure glove at second base. This game will mark his home debut for the Red Sox, but in the arc of baseball history it means a whole lot more.

The old ballpark on Lansdowne Street is crowded, unusual for a Tuesday, swollen to over twenty-one thousand by the throngs of African American fans out in the bleachers. They have come to see the rookie's first home game and cheer him on because he is the very first Black player to appear in a Red Sox uniform. The venerable organization has emerged from baseball's dark ages and is, surprisingly, the last big league team to sign a Black player. Boston, the oldest and one of the most progressive of American cities, where in 1770 British soldiers who, in fear for their lives, fired upon rebellious and boisterous Bostonians at the infamous massacre.

Boston, where William Lloyd Garrison held forth nightly in the 1830s and 1840s carrying the banner for the abolitionist movement. Boston, where in 1862, with the Union on the ropes and in desperate need of troops, Captain Robert Gould Shaw organized the legendary all-Black Fifty-Fourth regiment that fought gloriously in the Civil War. And Boston, where in 1974, after a court order that called for busing to achieve school desegregation, racial tension drove a wedge between citizens.

Pumpsie Green. Hitting the pitch into history.
African American Ethnic Sports Hall of Fame

Baseball had been integrated for twelve years, and some of the biggest stars in the game were Black. Trailblazer Jackie Robinson had retired in 1956, but southerners like Willie Mays, Henry Aaron, and Ernie Banks, and Californians like Frank Robinson and Vada Pinson, flourished, although almost exclusively in the National League. The Yankees, perennial pennant winners, had only one African American on their roster, catcher Elston Howard, who came aboard in 1955. Meanwhile, the Red Sox, who had not won a World Series since 1918 and would not win another one until 2004, were as white as a Robert Frost winter.

Across town at the Boston Garden, the multiracial Celtics, under the guidance of Red Auerbach, were building a sports dynasty the likes of which had never been seen anywhere, not even at Yankee Stadium. Nightly, Bill Russell, Bob Cousy, Sam Jones, K. C. Jones, and company would run their opponents off the parquet floor en route to one of the eleven NBA championships they would win between 1957 and 1969. Meanwhile, the rest of the world waited for the Red Sox to come around.

Finally, after all of his fellow millionaires saw the light that Branch Rickey shone brightly in their faces in 1947 when he made Jackie Robinson a Dodger, Red Sox owner Tom Yawkey capitulated. He had been accused of racism for allegedly passing up signing Mays and Robinson. But under pressure from the team, who needed a second baseman; the community; and all of baseball, the industrialist who owned the Red Sox for forty-four years, longer than any other owner in major league history, finally did the right thing. Boston baseball would never be the same.

"I was twenty-five, and my feeling was like any rookie just getting to the major leagues," Elijah "Pumpsie" Green reminisced in a lengthy 2008 interview with the authors, remembering that game like it was yesterday.

"I had butterflies, but I was playing a game I'd been playing all my life. All I had to do was convince myself to go out and play. That was the hardest part, but it got easier once I played a little while, fielded a couple of ground balls. I settled down a little bit.

"There were a lot of people at the park that night, folks that had never been to Fenway. About five thousand Black fans showed up that night, and they roped off centerfield because they were afraid something might happen. They had all come to see me, and I was nervous. But in the top of the first inning I turned a double play, so I felt good about that. I ran off the field into the dugout and got ready because I was leading off the bottom of the first.

"So I got my bat and helmet and walked up to home plate and got a standing ovation on my way there. It was deafening—I mean, they just stood—everybody. I said to myself, 'You can't strike out.' The first pitch, I took a called strike. The next pitch was a ball, outside. Here comes the third pitch, and I said to myself, if it's close, I'm swingin'. It was a breaking ball; I swung and hit a shot, high and deep off the left-center field wall. I left home plate running and slid into third base with a triple.

"Boy, that really felt good. I jumped up, took a deep breath, and got another standing ovation. It was great. But this little part wasn't over. Pete Runnels was up, and he hit a fly ball. I went back to third base and tagged up and ran to home plate, scoring standing up.

"The catcher suddenly called for the ball—he was saying that I didn't touch home plate! The manager said, 'Pumpsie, did you touch home plate?' To tell the truth, I didn't know, I was so excited. When they got the ball, he made his appeal, and the umpire called me safe—that was a big load off my mind. I'll never forget."

The rookie went on to have a fine day. But the first at bat was the one that mattered, and it wasn't just Pumpsie Green that scored in that inning. A weight the size of Fenway Park was lifted off the Red Sox, the city of Boston, and all of baseball, for the last holdouts, the Red Sox, had finally integrated its roster. And it was fitting that the fleet young Pumpsie, in his first at bat at Fenway, executed the most exciting play in baseball—he tripled off the Green Monster.

Elijah Green Jr. was born in the Dust Bowl in 1933 in the middle of the Depression.

"I was born in Boley, Oklahoma, in 1933," he began, "and I lived there until the age of nine, which was when we moved to California. It was a small, all-Black town out in the boondocks. I grew up working on the farm—cows, hogs, chickens, whatever. There were no white kids in the town, just a few Indian kids we played with."

The African American Registry lists Boley as a "FUBU" (for us, by us) town, established by Blacks who migrated from the South after slavery, hopeful of escaping discrimination and determined to make new lives for themselves.

The *Oklahoma Eagle* ran this story by Ken Raymond on June 2, 2017: "Boley was once the crown jewel of all the black towns in Oklahoma. Booker T. Washington came to Boley and deemed it the finest black town in the world—and he had literally been all around the world. Boley, its significance in commerce, its significance in education, parallels no other black town in the nation."

The decline of Boley was the result of several developments. One was the grandfather clause, a law that said you could only vote if your grandfather did; thus it took away Blacks' voting power. Soon there were only white people running an all-Black town. Then the Great Depression came in 1930, and it was a difficult time for Boley. By the time Pumpsie was born in 1933, the town was in full decline. The town never recovered, as many of its families were forced to leave to find work. Boley, once a thriving and vibrant city, is now nearly a ghost town, with only nine hundred residents.

For many people in that part of the country, their dream was to get out, move to California, and have a better life. Pumpsie's family did exactly that, and his parents both went to work in the Richmond, California, shipyards. In 1942, Richmond was mostly a white town, populated by folks who came out from the South and the Midwest before World War II.

"I had four brothers and I was the oldest," Pumpsie recollected. "Where I really grew up was in Richmond. As far as the racial thing goes, I've traveled all over the U.S. and the world, and my assessment of Richmond is that there isn't any place I've been that was more discriminatory, and I've been to Mississippi and Alabama.

"Playgrounds, parks, all kinds of things were not open to us. In those days, there was a beautiful baseball diamond at Nicholl Park, and we couldn't play there," Green said. He had lots of friends then, some of whom would remain friends for the rest of his life. One of them was a teammate on several baseball teams with Pumpsie.

"He was a great athlete," said his childhood friend Willie Reed in a recent conversation with the authors, "and he had a tremendous personality. Even as a kid, when he spoke he was serious."

Pumpsie, being the oldest son, was assigned responsibility at an early age. "I was the overseer of all my brothers. If any of them got in trouble, it was my fault. My folks taught us right from wrong. My mother was the boss; my father was the first mate. It was my responsibility to go get whoever was where they weren't supposed to be and bring them home."

He continued, "I went to class every day. I must have loved school because I never missed a day, even if I was feeling sick. I never missed a class. There was nothing else to do if you didn't go to school. I loved school so much that one morning I got up and went to school, and when I got there nobody was there because it was a holiday!

"My favorite subject was math—it was easy for me. I helped the other kids in math. I almost got in trouble once in junior high. The principal came in one day and saw me and said, 'What are you doing?' I said I'm doing my work. She said, 'You did all this?' I said, 'Yeah.' She asked me if I cheated. Finally the teacher came over and said, 'This is Pumpsie, and he's right where he's supposed to be.' I was mad, but I couldn't say anything, because back then if you did you got in trouble, and even if I didn't, I still had somebody to face at home."

For Pumpsie, playtime meant on the field or the court. He found his passion early on, one that would take him all over the country: sports. In the 1940s, boys played baseball in the spring and summer, football in the fall, and basketball in the winter. Some excelled.

"I liked all the sports," Green said. "I did my homework at school; if I had a paper or something, I did it at school. At my house, there wasn't enough space, time, or peace and quiet to get any schoolwork done. Every day after school I'd have practice and then come home for dinner."

In 1950, Pumpsie and his brothers commuted to school from neighboring Richmond to El Cerrito, a white community that has historically drawn from Richmond. After the war, there was a large influx of African Americans who came to work in the Richmond shipyards.

"It was mainly white students then," he recalled. "All the kids in South Richmond went to El Cerrito High because Richmond High didn't have enough room. We rode the bus. There was a policeman named Lonnie Washington who took me under his wing and taught me a lot. You could say he was my mentor."

Willie Reed remembered when Pumpsie joined the team as a junior. "When he joined we already had a shortstop, so the coach put him at first base, which was crazy because Pumpsie was already an incredible shortstop," Reed said. "But he never complained. I left for college, and the next year a new coach came in and immediately put Pumpsie at short."

Reed shared a funny story. "We went up to Canada that summer. We were in Medicine Hat, a beautiful town, and we went into a restaurant. Pumpsie looked over the menu and said, 'I'll have the Welsh rarebit,' not realizing that the dish was not rabbit. When the waitress brought out the food, Pumpsie saw a bowl of cheesy soup in front of him and said, 'I didn't order this—I asked for rabbit.' She politely said, 'Well, this is what you ordered.' He had lived in Oklahoma and wanted something familiar."

In 1947, when Pumpsie was thirteen, Jackie Robinson broke the color barrier.

"All the kids became Dodger fans," Green said, "so I became one too. But as far as I was concerned, baseball had already been integrated, because the [integrated] Oakland Oaks were my team, and I wanted to play for them when I was growing up. I wasn't thinking about the major leagues. Boston, New York—that was the other side of the world. The Oaks, the San Francisco Seals, they were right here. This was the major leagues as far as I knew.

"I played baseball and basketball at Contra Costa College, and then I signed with the Oaks, although I never got a chance to play with them. It was during the Korean War, and a good friend of mine, J. L. Woods, who I played with in high school, was sent over there and got killed the first day he was there, which was the last day of the war in 1953."

Pumpsie dealt with a physical condition his entire life.

"I went over to San Francisco for my physical, and they told me to get out and don't come back—I had a heart murmur. Growing up, my mother noticed something," he said. "She made me come home after school and lie down and rest every day. To this day, I still have to rest. The doctor would have me run around the whole block, come back and jump up and down a few times, and check my heart. One time they stopped me from playing baseball. I told them if I couldn't play baseball, then I didn't want to go to school."

In the early 1950s, the Oakland Oaks were in the Pacific Coast League, a landing ground for ballplayers either on their way up to or down from the big leagues. The manager was Augie Galan, who had played for the Chicago Cubs. Galan saw something in the speedy switch-hitting shortstop, and before Galan was fired in 1953, he signed Green to the Oaks. Pumpsie's dream had come true, but it didn't turn out the way he had envisioned it.

"My coach at Contra Costa, Gene Corr, got me a tryout with the Oaks. There were no agents then. They signed me, knowing they could sell me. But I never got to play for the Oaks."

He did play in Wenatchee, Washington, and Stockton, California, in the Oaks' minor league teams and had a fine year in 1955. That year the Red Sox, who needed middle infielders, bought his contract from the Oaks. In the 1950s, the major leagues had a multitiered minor league system. Hardly any players went to college, so the development took place in what was known as the farm system. Pumpsie paid his dues and worked his way through the minor leagues.

"The Red Sox wanted to send me to Montgomery, Alabama," Green recalled. "I told them I wasn't going because of all the racial problems that were going on. Earl Wilson, who later pitched for the Tigers, was the only other Black player in the organization at the time, and they wanted me to join him down there. My manager asked if I could stay in Stockton, so they let me stay. The next year, I went to the Red Sox single-A team in Albany; from there they moved me up to AA in Oklahoma City, in the Texas League.

"It was great because a lot of my relatives could see me. You know, hometown boy makes good and all that. I had met my wife, Marie, during college, and when I wasn't playing baseball, I spent time with her. We got married in 1957."

In 1958, Pumpsie was sent up to the Red Sox AAA club, the Minneapolis Millers. Among the future Hall of Famers who played for that team were Willie Mays, Orlando Cepeda, Hoyt Wilhelm, and Red Sox outfielders Carl Yastrzemski and Ted Williams. That first year in Minnesota, Pumpsie hit .253. The next year he posted a .320 average in ninety-eight games. The Red Sox had seen enough, and he was on his way to "the show."

"The Red Sox hadn't yet brought any Black players up," Green said, "and there were many times when people wouldn't let me forget it. I remember one guy would always come out and heckle me, saying, 'Green, you're not gonna play for the Red Sox. Who the hell do you think you are?'

"Gene Mauch was my manager at Minneapolis—he was a fiery son of a gun," Pumpsie said. "He taught me everything about baseball. What I remember is how he cared about me. One time in San Antonio a guy in the crowd was picking on me, yelling all kinds of racial insults. Gene told the owner of the team, 'If you don't get this SOB out of here, I'm pulling my whole team off the field!' Gene stuck up for me and always did the right thing."

When they traveled, everything was separate for the Black players—separate hotels, separate restaurants, and often they would have to stay in a separate town. When the team got into a town, they would have to take a bus or taxi over to the Black part of town to find lodging. It was the same for every Black ballplayer.

In this day of free agency, gargantuan contracts, cable television, watered-down pitching, luxury boxes, and, as many fans believe, the selling out of baseball to corporate greed, Pumpsie's story has a ring of nostalgia, although it's easy to romanticize about an era when you're not the one who had to deal with the long bus rides, low pay, and virulent racism. In July 1959, the Red Sox finally brought Pumpsie Green up.

"It was exciting and exhausting," he continued. "I was always being interviewed. We lived in Boston with our baby son. During the winter, I came back home to the East Bay and worked in the post office in Berkeley and Oakland. I didn't get any special treatment."

Pumpsie went on to play three and a half years in Boston, mainly as a utility infielder. With his speed, the Sox used him primarily as a pinch runner and a defensive replacement. Those were lean years for the Red Sox—they had a losing record each of the four years Green was on the team. There were a lot of good memories, but nothing matches that first at bat.

"I think that first night at Fenway was the highlight for me. I never really got that close to Billy Jurges or Mike Higgins (the managers during Pumpsie's tenure with Boston). But I did get close to a lot of guys on the team, like Ted Williams."

The legendary Williams was already forty years old when Pumpsie arrived and had really the only down year of his career in 1959. He came back with a fine season in 1960. Pumpsie concurs with many about Williams's place in the history of the game.

"I believe that he was the greatest hitter of all time, because he told me he was," laughed Pumpsie. "You could ask him something about hitting, and he'd sit down and talk to you as long as you would listen. Ted was a teacher—a good one.

"But I have to agree with those who say that he was the greatest. When he came up for his last at bat against Baltimore at Fenway, he went deep over the right field fence—a real long home run. The next inning, Mike Higgins had him go to the outfield and then come back out of the game so he could get a standing ovation. On his way back to the dugout, he ran past me laughing and said, 'Ain't this is a crock of shit.'"

Pumpsie was traded to the Mets after the 1962 season, the first season for the New York franchise, one in which they lost 120 games. They sent him down right away to the minor leagues, and when he came back he only appeared in seventeen games. That would be the last stop in the big leagues for Pumpsie.

Pumpsie reflected on his career: "I'm happy with what I did and when I did it. If I had to do it over again, I wouldn't change a thing. I'd do the same thing. I don't feel bad or sorry about anything that happened. I liked every situation I was in and the way I handled it."

Pumpsie Green left baseball for good at the end of the 1963 season, just before his thirtieth birthday. "I had a bum hip that was getting worse every time I played, and I was tired of all those cortisone shots I was getting. That was it. But I kept playing. Out of all the X-rays they took, they never found anything."

He worked for a while at the Alameda Naval Air Station, and then a job came up as student supervisor at Berkeley High. He stayed on and taught math during summer school. In his job, he did a lot of different things, such as keeping an eye on what was going on at the school.

"They had a rough time getting a coach for the baseball team," Green said, "and the principal came to me and asked me to coach, so I did that for eighteen years."

Berkeley is a town that has given the baseball world some great players. The legendary Billy Martin played there in the 1940s. Pumpsie coached a few in his time;

Claudell Washington, Ruppert Jones, and Glenn Burke all went to the pros. Burke was a trailblazer in his own right.

A gay man, he was the first professional athlete to come out of the closet. After that, he wound up on the Dodgers, where he ultimately left the team. But Burke's sexuality, which he steadfastly refused to deny, remained an issue, and after a knee injury he decided to quit the game. Sadly, his life spiraled downhill, and he died of AIDS in 1995.

Education is a theme of Pumpsie's life, and it is probably not a coincidence that he married an educator. His wife, Marie, taught school for many years in Oakland, teaching art, history, and other subjects. Pumpsie retired from the Berkeley School District in 1996 after about thirty years and moved to El Cerrito, close to his alma mater. Things have changed since he was a kid growing up in the 1940s.

"Most youngsters don't seem to appreciate school. When I was coming up, school was important," he continued, "but now there are a lot of kids who don't go. Society has changed. We're in a go, go, go society. The pressure on the kids is too much."

Pumpsie's younger brother Cornell was a basketball star in high school and then at Utah State. He didn't play football in college, but the Dallas Cowboys were so impressed with his athletic ability that they drafted him anyway. He played thirteen years as a defensive back for the Cowboys, going to the Pro Bowl five times and winning a Super Bowl in 1971. Cornell worked as a scout for the Cowboys from 1970 to 1979, then for the Denver Broncos from 1987 to 2013.

Another brother, Credell, played football at the University of Washington and was on a Husky team that became infamous for rebelling against the racist policies of Coach John Cherberg, who later became lieutenant governor of Washington. The outspoken Credell was a team leader. In 1955, as a junior halfback, Credell ran for 258 yards in a game. He was drafted by the Green Bay Packers in 1957 but had the misfortune of being selected behind another running back, Hall of Famer Paul Hornung.

"Someday I'll write a book and call it 'How I Got the Nickname Pumpsie' and sell it for one dollar, and if everybody who ever asked me that question buys the book, I'll be a millionaire," Pumpsie joked. "I've always had it, since I was real little, before I even saw a baseball. I don't know how I got it. I asked my mother, and she couldn't tell me. I didn't know what my real name was until I was much older. She never called me Elijah."

Pumpsie played during the golden era of baseball, before expansion, free agency, inflated salaries, and steroids tainted the innocence and purity of the game. He talked about the money ballplayers are making now. "I feel like they got a bird nest on the ground, and they should treat it with more respect. But that's not part of my life anymore. Baseball has overcome a lot of things; it's bigger than ever now."

When the African American Ethnic Sports Hall of Fame was established in 2000, Pumpsie was a member of the inaugural class, along with R. C. Owens, Willy T. Ribbs, Jamaal Wilkes, Joe Perry, Madeline Manning, Don Barksdale, Bob "Boomer" Brown, Jim Hines, Toni Stone, and Clem Daniels.

"Pumpsie had a terrific sense of humor," founder Arif Khatib said. "When I inducted him, I discovered while I was standing on the stage that my graphics person had misspelled his name in the souvenir program. It was spelled "Pimpsie," and he brought it to my attention when he mentioned it in his acceptance speech. It was very embarrassing, but he just looked at me and laughed along with over five hundred people in the room at the Claremont Hotel. Pumpsie remained my friend until his death, and he will be remembered as not only a great athlete but a better person."

The Honorable Nat Bates is the former mayor and currently vice mayor of the city of Richmond, California, and at ninety is the longest-living serving politician in the nation. He knew Pumpsie since they were in grade school and had these kind words to say about his old friend: "Pumpsie was not only an outstanding athlete but also a great and dear friend since our early childhood. He was also a terrific family man and will greatly be missed by those who knew him."

Willie Reed gave him a fitting tribute: "As long as I knew him, I never saw him angry."

On May 6, 2022, Nicholl Park in Richmond, where Pumpsie and his boyhood friends were not allowed to play, was renamed Willie Mays Park.

Elijah "Pumpsie" Green was a beautiful soul. He was a trailblazer, a professional ballplayer who, although he had a modest career, did something very special. But he was so much more than that. He was a family man known for his kind heart and gentle demeanor. Green passed away at the age of eighty-five on July 17, 2019, and left a loving family four generations deep, a wealth of friends, and a treasure trove of memories.

At 11:40 p.m., EST, on October 27, 2004, closer Keith Foulke gloved a soft grounder and underhanded it to first to complete a 3–0 shutout. Thus the Boston Red Sox, who the week before had engineered the most dramatic postseason comeback in the history of the game against their historic rival, the New York Yankees, put the finishing touches on their triumphant season with a sweep of the St. Louis Cardinals, throwing off the Curse of the Bambino, the Curse of Bill Buckner, and eighty-six years of anguish and frustration to win the World Series.

Meanwhile, in a quiet home in El Cerrito, California, a gray-haired former second baseman smiled. After all, it was his seventy-first birthday, and he couldn't have received a better present.

Godspeed, Elijah "Pumpsie" Green, a trailblazer with no regrets.

2

The Gold at the End of the Race

Alice Coachman

Alice Coachman made history in the 1948 Olympic Games high-jump competition, becoming the first Black woman to win an Olympic gold medal. Coachman had come from a poor background in Albany, Georgia, and dealt with the challenges of segregation and sexism in America that restricted her access to top-quality training facilities. But on her own, she improvised training tools and techniques that enabled her to achieve amazing success in the world of track and field. She won several titles in the 50- and 100-meter races and the 400-meter relay, and she was also an outstanding basketball player. But the high jump was her true calling; she won the American national title ten years in a row in the run-up to her 1948 Olympic victory.

Her gold medal was not just the first to be won by a Black woman—she was also the only American woman in track and field to win a gold medal at the 1948 Games. Four years later, she became the first Black female athlete to endorse an international product. Later she established a foundation to help support young athletes and retired Olympic veterans. She has been inducted into nine different halls of fame.

This is the story of one woman's rise from poverty to the greatest athletic stage in the world, and the grace, dignity, and pride with which she carried herself for sixty-six years after that triumph. In a 1985 interview with Washington University for their Black Champions series, Alice Coachman described that historic day in London in 1948:

"My Olympic coach said, 'You just like the rest of 'em [the other runners]; you gonna come up with nothin'.' She had wanted me to work out the day before, but I never worked out the day before a meet. I understood my routine because I had been on the All-American team for three years, and I was the only Black on that

Alice Coachman. The gold never gets old.
Courtesy of Richmond Davis

team. She kept fussin' and all, but I was talking to the man above, and I said, it is your will—let it be done. I went out there with my good luck charm, a lemon. I had carried a lemon around with me to every track and field event for eleven years. That's all it took—that and God's will.

"The other runners would eat chocolate bars to give them strength and energy, she said. But a lemon was mine. I had to do the high jump, and I had to go up and over, so I had to be light. I couldn't drink a lot of water like the other runners, so my mouth was dry. All I had to do was squeeze a drop of this lemon in my mouth. The English weather was cold and dry. I didn't know what was going on. You know, my coach had cussed me out before the meet. All the other girls had failed—there was not a second place then. I was the last one—the last hope."

In a tribute to her on Biography.com after she passed away in 2014, Coachman is quoted as saying, "I didn't know I'd won. I was on my way to receive the medal and I saw my name on the board, 'A. Coachman, U.S.A., Number One.' I went up, stood there, and they started playing the national anthem. It was wonderful to hear," Coachman remembered. "And of course I glanced over into the stands where my coach was, and she was clapping her hands. I had accomplished what I wanted to do. I've always believed that I could do whatever I set my mind to do. From the very first medal I ever won in 1939, my mama used to stress being humble. She said, 'You're no better than anyone else.'"

Today, Albany, Georgia, population seventy-five thousand, located in the center of Southwest Georgia, is home to the Civil Rights Institute, celebrating Albany's African American civil rights legacy. The institute is next door to the Mount Zion Baptist Church, site of several of Dr. Martin Luther King Jr.'s most memorable speeches. And if you visit on the second Saturday of the month, you'll hear the authentic songs of the civil rights era performed by the SNCC Freedom Singers, a group formed in 1962 to share songs of freedom.

But Albany, which is 75 percent African American, despite being rich in culture and history, has the highest concentrated poverty rate of any metro area in Georgia and one of the highest of any metro area nationwide. There are nine neighborhoods in the city with poverty rates of 40 percent and up; they are home to more than one-third of the 34,600 people living below the poverty line.

In 1923, Albany was a region still closely tied to America's early Native American culture. When in 1831 Andrew Jackson ordered the five tribes of the region sent to what would ultimately be Oklahoma on the infamous and brutal Trail of Tears, many of the Native Americans on that horrible journey were displaced from their ancestral homes in Georgia—including some of Alice Coachman's ancestors. Albany was also the heart of the Confederacy, the site of many large plantations that enslaved generations of people who toiled the cotton fields.

In 1930, a young man was born there who would put Albany on the map—his name was Ray Charles. Downtown is the Ray Charles Memorial that features a life-size statue of the "Genius." But before Ray Charles broke out nationally as a star in the early 1950s, a young woman from Albany burst onto the scene in 1948, winning an international athletic award that signified she was the best in the world at what she did. This is her story.

Alice Coachman was born on November 9, 1923, in the middle of the Jim Crow era, the fifth of ten children born to Fred Coachman, a plasterer, and Evelyn Coachman. The family worked hard, and young Alice kicked in with all the chores. Her daily routine included going to school and supplementing the family income by picking cotton, supplying corn to local mills, and picking plums and pecans to sell. But when she wasn't working, Alice loved to play outside. It became apparent early on that Alice was exceptionally athletic; she could run faster and jump higher than all of her friends, male or female.

When she was a child, girls did not for the most part compete in sports. In fact, most people, among them Alice's mother, thought women should not participate in sports at all. Alice's father also subscribed to these ideas and discouraged his daughters from playing sports. He sometimes whipped Alice for pursuing athletics, preferring that she sit on the front porch and look "dainty."

But this did not stop young Alice. Not only did she run; she played baseball with the boys. Growing up, she did not think of pursuing athletics as a career; she enjoyed music and dance and daydreamed about what it would be like as a musician or dancer, like her idols, the great jazz saxophonist Coleman Hawkins and child movie star Shirley Temple. It was two strong women, her fifth-grade teacher at Monroe Street School, Cora Bailey, and her aunt, Carrie Spry, who encouraged her to continue running.

By seventh grade, she was one of the best athletes in Albany, boy or girl. But she was not allowed to use any of the equipment or facilities for training or competing that the white kids used. So she improvised and trained on her own, using what was available to her, running barefoot on dusty roads to improve her stamina and using sticks and rope to practice the high jump.

"You had to run up and down the red roads and the dirt roads," Coachman said in a 1995 interview with William Rhoden of the *New York Times*. "You went out there in the fields, where there was a lot of grass and no track."

Added to the list of challenges was her status as a female athlete during a time of widespread opposition to girls and women in sports. But that did not stop Alice.

While still in junior high school, the track coach at Madison High School in Albany saw her potential and invited her to join the track team there. She enrolled at Madison in 1938. The coach saw that Alice was an outstanding high jumper as well as an excellent sprinter, so when the team went to the Tuskegee Relays, Alice participated in the high jump and won. They called her name after each jump, she kept jumping, and she kept winning.

A coach at Tuskegee asked her parents if Coachman could train with their high school team during the summer. So in 1939, at the age of sixteen, she transferred to Tuskegee Preparatory School. This would be the start of a celebrated athletic career.

Tuskegee University, founded in 1881, is one of the oldest and most well known historically Black colleges and universities (HBCUs) in the United States. It is one of only eight American colleges that start in kindergarten and go all the way through to graduate school.

The school is noted for its rigorous academic standards, diverse curriculum, and famous alumni, among them Booker T. Washington, who served as the first president of the institute from 1881 to 1915. Other alumni include George Washington Carver, scientist, botanist, educator, and inventor whose studies and teaching revolutionized agriculture in the southern United States, and the highly decorated, celebrated Tuskegee Airmen, legendary pilots of World War II.

At Tuskegee, Alice had a work-study scholarship that required her to have jobs while studying and training. Tuskegee was more than just a school for young Alice. In a recent interview, her son Richmond Davis described the significance of Tuskegee in his mother's life.

"She came from a poor family, and when she got to Tuskegee she learned the social parts of life there. The teachers gave her shoes and clothes," he said, "and after she came back from the Olympics they treated us well. For the rest of her life she stayed in touch with her good friends from school. She met her second husband, my father, Nathan Davis, during that time. He was in the military. I was born there, as was my sister. Alice really loved it there."

Coachman said much later that track was her key to getting a degree, meeting great people, and opening a lot of doors in high school and college. In 1943, at nineteen, Coachman entered the Tuskegee college division to study dressmaking while continuing to compete for the school's track and field and basketball teams. Her work-study tasks included cleaning and maintaining sports facilities as well as mending uniforms.

As a member of the "Tuskegee Ten" women's track team, she won four national championships for sprinting and high-jumping. During this time, Coachman competed in the Amateur Athletic Union's (AAU) Women's National Championships. Although she was an outstanding sprinter, she soon found that her best event was the high jump, which requires great speed when doing the run-up to the bar. Incredibly, she broke the college and national high-jump records while competing barefoot. Her unusual jumping style was a combination of straight jumping and Western roll techniques.

Coachman went on to graduate with a degree in dressmaking from the institute in 1946. The following year she continued her studies at Albany State College.

A fierce competitor, Coachman dominated the AAU outdoor high-jump championship from 1939 through 1948, winning an uncanny ten national championships in a row. In addition to those accomplishments, she won national championships in the 50-meter dash, the 100-meter dash, and the 400-meter relay with the Tuskegee team. During the same period, Coachman won three conference championships playing guard on the Tuskegee women's basketball team and went on to compete in track for Albany State College (now Albany State University).

People around her were understandably trying to convince her to try out for the Olympics. She was one of the best track and field competitors in the country. Yet, for many of those years, the Olympics were out of reach. In 1940 and 1944, when she was at her peak, the Games were canceled due to World War II.

Sportswriter Eric Williams praised Coachman for the Black Action Sports Network in 2006: "Had she competed in those canceled Olympics, we would probably be talking about her as the No. 1 female athlete of all time."

When the Games were back on in 1948, Coachman was still reluctant to try out for the team. Pushed by friends, family, and coaches, she eventually attended the trials at Northwestern University in Evanston, Illinois, and despite competing with a back injury, she set a new USA high-jump record with a jump of 5'4¾".

Coachman's first opportunity to compete on the global stage came at the 1948 Summer Olympic Games in London. An outgoing young woman, while on the boat over to England with her fellow athletes, to keep nervous young spirits light, she did a dance for the guests on the ship.

On a rainy afternoon at Wembley Stadium in London in August 1948, in the high-jump final in front of eighty-six thousand people, Coachman represented the USA, competing for Olympic gold. She became the gold medalist when she cleared the 5'6⅛" bar on her first attempt.

Her nearest rival, Great Britain's hometown heroine Dorothy Tyler, matched Coachman's jump, but only on her second try, thus giving the gold medal to Coachman. It was a new Olympic record. King George VI of Great Britain put the medal around her neck. She was invited aboard a British Royal yacht. Coachman remembered the moment long afterward.

"Many people will tell you Wilma Rudolph was the first Black woman to win a gold medal—it's not true," she said in the 1995 *New York Times* interview, referring to Rudolph's three gold medals in the sprints at the Rome Olympics. "She came on the scene 12 years later. But she was on television, so I understood."

As the gold medal winner in the high jump, when Coachman returned to the United States she was a celebrity. Soon after she had met President Harry Truman and former First Lady Eleanor Roosevelt, Count Basie, the famous jazz musician, threw her a party. Alice Coachman came home to what she thought would be a hero's welcome. She rode in a 175-mile motorcade from Atlanta to her hometown of Albany, where the town came out for a parade in her honor. And there was an "Alice Coachman Day" in Georgia to celebrate her accomplishment.

But these celebrations occurred in the segregated Deep South. In the Albany auditorium where she was honored, whites and African Americans had to sit in separate sections. The white mayor of Albany at the time, a man named J. W. Smith, sat on the stage with Coachman but refused to shake her hand. Coachman was not permitted to speak at the ceremony. And, adding insult to injury, she had to leave her own celebration by a side door.

The town's problem with Alice had nothing to do with her character. It was the color of her skin. Alice Coachman was a colorless world-class athlete, an Olympic champion, who had returned to the segregated South. She was not surprised at the behavior of city officials during the era of Jim Crow; she was all too familiar with unjust treatment. Still, when Albany officials snubbed her after her victory, it hurt, especially in light of the fact that she had received her gold medal in London from English king George VI.

Alice traveled all over Europe after 1948, competing in exhibitions and meets. Her Tuskegee education proved invaluable; the social skills she acquired there stood her in good stead overseas. But upon her arrival back in the United States, she felt like a stranger in her home country. The South in 1948 had yet to undergo any cultural shift. Alice recalled that she often got treated badly.

"To come back home to your own country, your own state and your own city, and you can't even get a handshake from the mayor? It wasn't a good feeling," she told the *Times* in 1995.

Some whites in the city were supportive, but they did not show that publicly. At a party at her godfather's house, she received gifts and flowers from well-wishers, but many of the packages arrived with no cards or names attached. Coachman said those came from white people.

Growing up in the segregated South, Alice Coachman overcame discrimination and unequal access to inspire generations of other Black athletes to reach their potential. At a time when there were few high-profile Black athletes beyond Jackie Robinson and Joe Louis—and literally none of them women—Alice Coachman became a pioneer. She led the way for female African American Olympic track stars like Wilma Rudolph, Evelyn Ashford, Florence Griffith Joyner, and Jackie Joyner-Kersee.

In fact, in the years since her Olympic victory, Black women have made up a majority of the U.S. women's Olympic track and field team, as well as her other sport, basketball, where they dominate the WNBA. In her July 15, 2014, obituary in the *Telegraph Online*, looking back on her legacy, her feelings were made clear. "I think I opened the gate for all of them," she reflected. "Whether they believe that or not, they should be grateful to someone in the Black race that was able to do these things."

"Ms. Coachman was a true trailblazer," said Dr. John Carlos, 1968 Olympic gold medalist, when interviewed in 2022 by the authors of this book. "She also went on to win the number one medal. Ms. Coachman didn't have a machine behind her like some white athletes, and didn't receive proper recognition when she returned home. She's partially responsible for women participating in sports. I was not personally influenced by her because of the different times, but I was always proud of her because she was able to overcome many odds.

"I applaud and respect the fact that she had to pretty much compete against herself because she could not compete against others during that time. I met her at the '96 Olympics in Georgia, and it occurred to me that she was from Georgia and did not receive the accolades she earned. She should have been held in much higher esteem because long before the Olympics in Georgia, she was representing the state on the international stage. And to some extent, she was responsible for Georgia's recognition in the Olympics and Atlanta hosting the Games in '96. In fact, I don't think any state gave a Black woman the recognition they deserved."

Alice was appreciative of her historic role. In her July 15, 2014, obituary in the *Washington Post*, she was quoted as saying, "I made a difference among the Blacks, being one of the leaders. If I had gone to the Games and failed, there wouldn't be anyone to follow in my footsteps. It encouraged the rest of the women to work harder and fight harder."

Coachman's athletic career ended when she was just twenty-four. She had two children during her first marriage to N. F. Davis, which ended in divorce. Her second husband, Frank Davis, preceded her in death.

She faded from public view after the Olympics, but her pride remained undiminished. She completed her degree at Albany State College, where she had enrolled in 1947. She graduated with a BS in home economics and a minor in science in 1949. She became an elementary and high school physical education teacher and track coach. There were many coaching opportunities for her in other parts of Georgia, and schools recruited her, but she wasn't interested in moving. She dedicated the rest of her life to her family, education, and the Job Corps.

In 1952, Coachman became the first Black female athlete to endorse an international consumer brand. Her son Richmond Davis was born in 1953 and spent much of his childhood in Atlanta. In his interview with the authors, Davis shared his recollections of that time.

"You know, kids of famous athletes, they are your parents first, so I didn't regard my mom as this international Olympic star—even though that was who she was. There were all kinds of famous people in Atlanta in the 1960s—civil rights leaders like Martin Luther King Jr., who I saw a lot. Also, there was a lot of jazz in the house. It was a huge part of my childhood—I was fortunate to get exposed to lots of people," he said.

Alice Coachman was inducted into nine halls of fame, including the National Track and Field Hall of Fame in 1975. In 1979 she was inducted into the Georgia Sports Hall of Fame. During the 1996 Summer Olympic Games in Atlanta, Coachman was honored as one of the one hundred greatest Olympians. She was an honorary member of Alpha Kappa Alpha Sorority, inducted in 1998. In 2002, she was designated a Women's History Month honoree by the National Women's History Project, and in 2004 she was inducted into the U.S. Olympic Hall of Fame.

In 1994, she started the Alice Coachman Track and Field Foundation, a nonprofit organization that provides assistance to young athletes and helps former Olympic athletes adjust to life after the Games. In her hometown of Albany, Alice Avenue and Coachman Elementary School are named in her honor.

She was an inspiration to many. In the *New York Times* 1995 interview, she exhorted young athletes to never give up, saying that "when the going gets tough and you feel like throwing your hands in the air, listen to that voice that tells you 'keep going, hang in there.' . . . Guts and determination will pull you through."

"I was from the South," Coachman continued, "and you had to do the best you could. If I had gone to the Games and failed, there wouldn't be anyone to follow in my footsteps."

When she was inducted along with twelve other Olympians to the African American Ethnic Sports Hall of Fame in 2004, Arif Khatib described meeting her.

"She was a fun-loving woman who enjoyed life. She shared with me the inequities of the time. She was well-liked and respected by her teammates. Mal Whitfield often spoke of their friendship. She was a lovely, funny person. When I visited her, she kept everything in the kitchen—papers, files, books, memorabilia," he joked, "not just food."

Alice Coachman died in her hometown of Albany, Georgia, on July 14, 2014, of cardiac arrest after suffering from respiratory problems. She had a stroke a few months prior, for which she received treatment from a nursing home. She was ninety years old.

Her legacy as a runner is secure. But it is her legacy as a proud African American woman, a trailblazer who set an example for others to follow, that must be honored and not forgotten. Many of the people she inspired had kind and respectful words to say about Alice.

Tommie Smith, 1968 Olympics gold medalist, lifetime social activist, and writer, had this to say about her: "She opened doors that no one else could open, and she literally started the liberation of women in sports. Had it not been for the Alice Coachmans in society, especially in our sport, track and field, I could have never been, because I would have had no portal to come through. Her mother looked at her from the opposite end and said, 'You can't do this; you're a woman, and you have to be more ladylike.' When she jumped, she used the scissors move, which meant her head was higher than any other part of her body. She was mighty in her ways."

Another trailblazer who knows something about courage in the face of all odds described how Coachman's achievements were more significant than just an Olympic gold medal.

"She was the first. That door opened for others to come along. We always need that door just open a little bit, and we'll push through. Alice Coachman was a forerunner—literally and figuratively—and exemplifies what's possible despite all kinds of limitations," said Minnijean Brown-Trickey when talking about Coachman in *Gold Medal Moments*, a video produced by Team USA. Trickey was a civil rights leader and a member of the Little Rock Nine, who desegregated Little Rock Central High School in 1957.

Trickey added, "The period in the '40s must have been nearly impossible. Everything was segregated—and I mean seriously segregated. I admire her willingness to go forward despite criticism. Historically Black colleges were really important in providing opportunities for people in sports. She was interested in education and knew it was a space where she could actually practice her sport. She should be well known and talked about and discussed for all young women, for all young people, for those are the stories we need to have as part of our litany of who we are as a nation."

Alice's son Richmond summed it up well: "My mother was a true American success story—she didn't let obstacles get in her way."

3

"If Pete Brown Ain't Coming, I Ain't Coming"

Pete Brown

Pete Brown is little known by most people, including those folks you'd think would know him, that is, fellow African American golfers. The question was posed recently to several, and none had ever heard of him. But he created a legacy for himself in the history of golf and American sport.

Charlie Sifford was the first Black golfer to play in a PGA tournament, but Brown was the first to win a PGA tournament. In 1963, Pete joined the tour, and in 1964 he became the first African American golfer to bring home a PGA title when he won the Waco Turner Invitational. In 1970, he earned his second PGA victory at the 1970 Andy Williams San Diego Open at Torrey Pines. He played on the PGA tour for seventeen years and also won twelve other non-PGA tournaments.

It was 1962, at the Michigan Open at Farmington Country Club, a course that doesn't exist anymore, only a year after the Caucasian-only clause was eradicated from the PGA of America bylaws, and it was the first year that Blacks were allowed in the event. Pete Brown had posted a final round score of 68 and was preparing to celebrate a close, hard-fought victory. He was about to share a beer with friends in the clubhouse when he was suddenly summoned to the first tee for a play-off.

"I was at the tee," recalled his wife, Margaret Brown, in the 2021 article "Remembering Pete Brown—The Man Who Deflected Hate and Won Many Hearts," by Bob Denney for PGA Championship News. "So Pete steps up to put his tee in the ground and adjust his ball. Just then, from across the fence, I could see some young men by a pickup truck. One of them yells, 'Hey, [N-word]! What are *you* doing up there?' Well, there were people all around the tee, and everyone got so quiet you could have heard a pin drop. Everybody just froze. Pete just backed off the ball, tossed his club on the ground, and started laughing."

Pete Brown. Joe Louis's favorite golfer.
African American Ethnic Sports Hall of Fame

The crowd, Margaret said, "was like, 'Okay, we can breathe again.' And they all started laughing, and now everybody was pulling for Pete. He steps back up and knocks that ball right down the fairway. I remember people saying, 'What a man, what a man!'"

But there was more. The same hecklers traveled down a road next to the first fairway. Brown had hit his approach to within ten feet and was facing a winning birdie putt.

"Hey, [N-word], what are you doing?" the same hateful voice yelled out. Brown shook his head, regrouped, and missed the putt. The play-off went to the par three third hole, and Pete Brown won it by sinking an eight-foot putt. As he picked up his ball out of the cup, he looked up and smiled.

When Tiger Woods won his first major championship at the 1997 Masters, finishing twelve strokes ahead of runner-up Tom Kite, he was standing on the shoulders of a few men who came before him. One was Charlie Sifford, the first African American golfer to play on the PGA tour.

Another was a little-known golfer from Mississippi, born in the middle of the Great Depression, forty years before Tiger, who was the first African American golfer to win a PGA tournament. When he was nineteen, he was stricken with a mysterious form of polio, but with the help of boxing legend Joe Louis, he recovered fully and had a long and fruitful career as a golfer. Along the way he made hundreds of friends and left behind a legacy of class, character, perseverance, and pride. His name was Pete Brown.

Pete Brown was born in Port Gibson, Mississippi, in 1935, the son of a sharecropper, and grew up in Jackson. He was a caddy in his early years and gave golf lessons to family members as a teenager. A happy-go-lucky kid, there was one thing that bothered Pete: his birth name, Earlie. He hated it so much that when he was seven, he changed his name to Pete—in honor of his pet horse, Pete.

As a youngster, Pete chopped cotton and picked peas. The family moved to Jackson when he was ten, and he started hanging out at the Livingston Park golf course where he became a caddie, making fifty-five cents a round. Blacks were not allowed to play that course or any other in the city, but at night, Brown said he and the other teenage caddies would sneak out and play a few holes on the course.

Pete developed a love for the sport while working as a caddie. After high school he moved up to Detroit to become a pro golfer, but when he was nineteen he became sick, mysteriously losing control of his muscles. The doctors could not diagnose the cause. In the article "Breakthrough at Burneyville" by Mike McAllister for PGAtour .com, Brown said that at the time, "They told me if I did survive, I'd have to give up golf because I'd be in a wheelchair the rest of my life."

One day, boxing legend, Detroit native, and recreational golfer Joe Louis, along with young pro Charlie Sifford, visited the hospital to check on Brown. Brown did not recognize them, so Louis left an autographed picture on his bed. "The doctor saw that and told me I must be an important guy to have Joe Louis as a friend. Then they started treating me better."

Soon a diagnosis was made of nonparalytic polio, and the doctors had a plan for his recovery. It was grueling, but Brown was determined to get through it and play his beloved game again. He moved to Los Angeles, practiced incessantly, and in July 1963 received his PGA card.

Brown later talked about the influence the Brown Bomber had on the world of golf in the United States during the 1950s and 1960s. He said that Joe Louis gave him the opportunity to play in tournaments that were usually reserved for white people. During that time, the PGA had a clause that allowed only white players to play.

But Louis was able to play because they wanted him in the tournament as a draw. "They used to call and say they wanted Joe to come to the Pro Am," Brown said at his 2007 induction into the African American Ethnic Sports Hall of Fame. "Joe said he wouldn't come unless other Black golfers, including Ted Rhodes and Charlie Sifford, could play. Joe also said, 'If Pete Brown ain't coming, I ain't coming.' Since everybody wanted to see the champ, it helped all of the Black players."

Brown was given the chance to play in tournaments at various private country clubs because he had played on the PGA tour. When he was inducted into the African American Ethnic Sports Hall of Fame in Harlem, New York, in 2007, founder Arif Khatib recalled the event.

"When I inducted him (along with Emile Griffith, Lynette Woodard, E. B. Henderson, Lou Hudson, Willie O'Ree, Wilma Rudolph, Willie Thrower, and John Isaacs), it was the first opportunity for me to meet him in person," said Khatib. "We'd had many phone conversations, and I really liked him. When he arrived with his lovely wife Margaret and several of his daughters, the hotel came alive. We had a great time from then on until they returned home."

Brown spent much of his career deflecting hatred and racism. During a tournament in Florida, he slept in his car because of threats from the Ku Klux Klan. And once, playing in Ohio, he stepped outside the ropes to buy a hot dog; when he came back onto the course, a marshal refused to let him back across the rope until fellow professional Tom Weiskopf came over.

Both of his PGA wins came down to the wire. Brown was the second African American to receive a PGA Tour card in 1963, following Charlie Sifford. Pete Brown's breakthrough moment happened in 1964 when he won the Waco Turner Open in Oklahoma by one stroke, rallying from behind against Dan Sikes. The tournament's namesake was a millionaire Oklahoma oilman with a passion for golf who carried two .45 revolvers on his belt during the open and demanded that the gallery behave and refrain from any display of intolerance that might be directed at Pete Brown.

While Brown was winning in Oklahoma, Margaret was in Los Angeles, pregnant with their youngest of six daughters, Tracie. That evening, after a one-stroke victory over Dan Sikes, he called her from his hotel room. Denney's 2021 article for PGA news described the call:

"Well, I won a tournament for you, and I want to see the kids," Pete said. It took a while for that to sink in. "That's wonderful," Margaret replied; "quit lying to me." "No, I won the tournament," Pete said. "I made history."

Picking out the best golfing day of his life was easy for Pete Brown. That would be the Sunday in February 1970 when he charged down the stretch of the Andy Williams San Diego Open at Torrey Pines to beat a pair of legends. His victory remains one of the most dramatic in the tournament's history.

He later recalled that he nearly didn't enter in San Diego because he was playing so poorly, and his prospects for winning looked dismal when he trailed by eleven shots after the first round, ten following the second, and seven going into Sunday. The leaders in front of Brown were Tony Jacklin, the reigning British Open champion who would go on to win the U.S. Open that year, and Jack Nicklaus, who had won seven majors that year en route to his record-holding eighteen and was the defending champion at Torrey Pines. Pete Brown erased the deficit on the first nine holes on Sunday with a 31.

"When I got up that morning, my wife and some friends talked to me, and for some reason I felt very relaxed right from the start," Denney recounted Brown's memory of that special day. "I'd never had a feeling like that before or since."

He birdied holes 10, 12, and 13, and although he bogeyed 15 and three-putted for par at 18, he still finished the round of 65, which was one off the course record at the time. Nicklaus was out when he surprisingly missed a four-foot putt for a birdie on 18. Jacklin tied Pete with a birdie. On the first play-off hole, number 15, Jacklin drove behind a tree, and his approach hit a branch and dropped straight down. Brown made par to win the $30,000 first prize.

Despite that victory, Brown didn't get an invitation to the Masters, just as his longtime friend Charlie Sifford hadn't in 1967 or 1969 when he won tour events. In those days, tour winners didn't get automatic invitations. At the time, if you played well, the former champions could invite a player they thought "deserved it." And if your name wasn't on that list, you didn't play.

Throughout his career, he was known for his calm, cool, upbeat demeanor, both on and off the links. Also from the 2021 PGA news story, Bob Goalby, the 1968 Masters champion, said of his friend, "Pete didn't let anything bother him; he never got too high or too low."

Pete Brown was the four-time USG National Open champion, a four-time Long Star Open champion, and a three-time North & South champion.

Pete's favorite course was the first golf club in America that was founded, built, owned, and operated by an African American: Clearview Golf Club in Canton, Ohio. Margaret recalled that Pete loved to play at the only Black owned and operated golf club at the time in America. Clearview was built by William Powell in 1946 and is still the only course that was designed, built, owned, and operated by an African American. It was named a National Historic Site by the Department of the Interior in 2001 and is managed today by his son Larry.

His daughter, Dr. Renee Powell, is the LPGA/PGA head golf professional at Clearview, where she's keeping her father's legacy of "Golf for Everyone" alive. Renee's work extends throughout her community as a member of several boards, including the Pro Football Hall of Fame.

Renee Powell is the second African American woman to play on an LPGA Tour, and as a tour player she competed in more than 250 professional tournaments and won the 1973 Kelly Springfield Open in Brisbane, Australia. She is also the first woman to compete in a men's tour, and she beat several men in a tournament held in Kenya. In February 2015, Renee became one of seven female members, and the first and only African American female member, of the Royal and Ancient Golf Club in St. Andrews, Scotland.

Margaret Brown remembered Clearview: "Pete would play at the club and would go fishing in one of the lakes on the property. Mr. Powell said only Pete would be able to fish in the ponds. I would hit balls with him, and one time I made a hole in one and won a set of golf clubs, but I didn't keep them and never really got into the game. But I remember how much fun it was to get that hole in one!"

Pete and Margaret are the proud parents of six daughters. One time, Sheila, the second youngest, then six years old, was watching her dad on the screen. Again from Bob Kenney's piece for PGA news: "Sheila asked everyone to be quiet, and to let the announcer speak. 'Here comes Pete Brown, one of the nicest men alive.' 'Hey, momma,' said Sheila, "Why do they always say Daddy is the nicest man alive? Aren't all the other golfers nice?' Margaret just blurted out, 'Sure they are, honey. But your daddy has that sneaky smile that wins your heart.'"

Pete Brown made 365 career starts on the PGA Tour. When he was older, Pete played in the Senior PGA Tour. When back pain began forcing him out of tournaments, he began running a driving range in Los Angeles. A year after a fire destroyed the Browns' home, he got a job as the head pro at Madden Golf Course in Dayton, Ohio, where he stayed for twenty-one years, retiring in 2004.

Brown endured eleven strokes and congestive heart failure but always bounced back. "One year, Pete was told that surgery couldn't be performed because they were afraid he would never survive it," said Margaret at the 2007 Hall of Fame ceremony. "Pete said, 'Oh, come on. Let's go for it.' The doctor looked at me, and I said, 'Well, I'm headed to a little room and do some praying.' Pete survived that to live several more years. After that surgery, all the nurses and doctors called him 'The Miracle Man.'"

His old friend, golfer Jim Dent, offered Pete and Margaret his second home in Evans, Georgia, near Augusta, far away from the cold Ohio winters. They lived there from 2012 to 2015, when Pete passed away at the age of eighty.

In 2019, Jackson Municipal Golf Course was renamed the Pete Brown Golf Facility. "He's their first African American golfer," said Margaret. "I was talking to one of our daughters a while back, and she said, 'Daddy sure made a lot of history, didn't he?'"

Margaret talked about how Pete would hit drives, and she would go ahead of him to be close to his golf ball and wait until it finished bouncing and rolled to a stop. "By doing this, I could keep people from stepping on or moving the ball, which they would do. That used to happen to him all the time."

In 2020, Pete was inducted into the Mississippi Sports Hall of Fame. Margaret said to the paper *Mississippi Today*, "This award means a lot to me, and it would mean a whole lot to Pete. I wish he was here, and I wish he had lived to enjoy this, but it's better late than never. He's looking down, smiling and saying Amen."

It's a fair bet to guess that wherever Pete Brown is, nobody is stepping on or moving the ball. The fairways are smooth and wide; his drives are long, straight, and true; the greens are lush, with an emerald hue; and the breaks are gentle as he calmly takes the putter from his bag, smiles, and sinks another birdie.

4

Time to Play by "the Rule"

Spencer Haywood

It was 1970, and after one year of the young player tearing up the old American Basketball Association, the big boys came calling. In a brazen move, NBA Seattle Supersonics owner Sam Schulman signed Spencer Haywood to a six-year, $1.5 million contract, ignoring the rule that a player cannot join the league until he is four years out of high school. As a result, the NBA threatened to disallow the contract and implement various sanctions against the Sonics.

"Sam Schulman stepped up," Spencer Haywood remembered like it was yesterday in a 2020 phone interview. "He wanted me to play for him, so he drafted me knowing it was against the rule. Sam knew that it wasn't right to prevent somebody from making a living, especially someone like me who had a large family that needed the money. So he put up the money for all the legal work and paid the legal bills all the way to the Supreme Court. California governor Pat Brown was on my legal team. Sam was a father figure to me. He said, 'This man is my son. I love him.'"

On December 30, 1970, Schulman signed Haywood. The NBA sued—and they ultimately lost. In March 1971, the Supreme Court ruled in a 7–2 decision against the NBA, establishing what would become known as the "hardship rule."

"Curt Flood came right on my heels," Spencer said. Flood refused his trade while the NBA case was in the courts. "And when I won that case, I won it for everybody that came after me. I cleaned it up for baseball, football, and basketball. A guy like LeBron, he didn't go to college. Without *my* rule, he would have missed out on $200 million, four years on his stats, four years of this life as an NBA player. Moses Malone, Kevin Garnett, all of them. And Michael Jordan, Steph Curry, and all these huge 'one and done' deals? Never would have happened."

Spencer Haywood. He stood up to the NBA. *Courtesy of the Michigan Sports Hall of Fame*

Spencer joined the Sonics in March 1971 and played the final thirty-three games of the season, averaging over twenty points and twelve rebounds despite the layoff. "My first year was hard. Being in the NBA was a war," he remembered. "People threw bottles at me, spit on me, called me every name in the book, but I was built for all the abuse, because of where I came from."

The Cincinnati Royals kicked him out of the arena and into the snow. Opposing players delivered elbows to Haywood's jaw. "Chet Walker (a Hall of Fame player, then with the Chicago Bulls) and the Bulls even sued me for $600,000 for causing him an injury *when I wasn't even in the game*," said Haywood. "Other players asked me, 'How do you take this shit?' But I was from Silver City, Mississippi—it just rolled off my back."

Scoop Jackson of ESPN quoted the late Kobe Bryant talking to HBO's *Real Sports* in his 2015 piece titled "It's Time to Honor Spencer Haywood's Impact on Hoops and History": "He pioneered this whole movement," Kobe said. "He was the first one to fight for what he believed in. And it's because of him. He's opened up the doors for guys like me, Kevin Garnett, Tracy McGrady, and LeBron James. It all started with him."

In a conversation with Spencer Haywood, the NBA Hall of Famer and trailblazer spoke candidly about his life and career and his feelings about how professional basketball has a chance to get it right, to give credit where credit is due after decades of ignoring his role and how it reshaped the economic and competitive landscape of pro sports.

"I'm tired of them calling it all these other names. They should call it the Spencer Haywood Rule," he said, referring to the landmark 1971 decision that forever altered the structure of the amateur draft for pro sports, the Supreme Court ruling against the NBA's old requirement that a player may not be drafted by an NBA team unless he waited four years (which meant playing at the college level in most cases) following his graduation from high school. The court granted an injunction that allowed Haywood to play for the Seattle Supersonics in the NBA and forbade the NBA from sanctioning the Seattle team.

"I mean, they have the Larry Bird Rule, from 1983 [which says teams can exceed the salary cap to re-sign their own player if they match an offer by another team] and the Oscar Robertson Rule [from 1976, which eliminated the reserve clause binding a player to one team for life, and was the first step toward free agency in the NBA], but the ruling by the Supreme Court in my favor was more important than both of those. Without that ruling, none of the players who came right out of high school, or did not complete four years of college—and that would be almost all of them these days—would not have made the millions they're making."

But before he expanded on that subject, Spencer Haywood wanted to give some personal background to help illustrate where he was literally coming from, and how it shaped him as an individual and an athlete, to help understand not just the details and markers of his bravery and longtime commitment to the cause of justice and fairness—and the need to give credit where credit is due—but the why of it.

"I see changes are similar to what I had to go through," Haywood said when asked about the tumultuous events happening today in sports and the racial landscape of America. "And I tell young people coming up, especially athletes, learn your history."

Spencer Haywood has a unique history to say the least. He shared some of his experiences growing up in Silver City, in the Mississippi delta, in the far western part of the state. When he was born in 1949, the population was 382; now it's 282. The 1950s in the South was a period that many Americans mistakenly believe was far removed from the old ways—slavery, cotton picking, and a way of life that no longer exists. Spencer is living proof that time, in many ways, had stood still.

"Starting as a little boy, I picked cotton on a farm for two dollars a day. My whole family, we worked from sunup to sundown, and all we ate on a break was rotten watermelon from our garden," he said. "Picking, chopping, and planting—that taught me how to work hard; my goal at that time was to be the best cotton picker in Mississippi. I look back at my life.

"I filled up one-hundred-pound bags of cotton, and my legs and calves got bigger. Then I had to put the bag on my back, walk almost a mile back to the trailer, weigh it, dump it, and start all over again." The youngest of eight children, he never met one of his parents. "My father passed away from a heart attack while my mother was carrying me," he said.

"So when I got to playing basketball, it was like being freed out of Parchman, the worst prison and worst cotton field in the world," he said. Parchman Farm is the infamous Mississippi state penitentiary whose name is synonymous with punishment and brutality. Over the years it has housed John Lewis, Stokely Carmichael, James Farmer, and blues singers Bukka White and Son House.

"School was secondary," he said. "At thirteen, I was the main earner for my family. By that time I was picking up two-hundred-pound bags of cotton for four dollars a day." When he was fourteen, he was working as a caddy at the local country club. A racist prank resulted in him being accused of trying to steal a quarter; he was punched in the face, fought back, and was thrown in jail. He was afraid that he might be facing a long stint in Parchman. His mother made sure that never happened.

"My mother said to me, 'Whatever happens, you got to get out of here because you have something special to give to the world. You're my baby and I gotta get you out of here. You're different.' So we gathered all of our money and I caught a bus up north."

After a brief stay in Fort Wayne, Indiana, he eventually arrived in Detroit and was taken in by longtime Pershing High basketball coach Will Robinson, who became like a father to the young man, eventually co-adopting him.

"I was playing a game I loved two hours a day. I was used to working twelve. I had endurance and discipline and a great work ethic from picking cotton. And I said to myself, 'I'm a basketball player—I want to play!' God trained me for basketball. I was stronger than others, and I had endurance and discipline. That's what transformed me into this great player," said Haywood. "So here I am, from Silver City, Mississippi, and I win a state Michigan Class A title, the city of Detroit's first in thirty-five years. My first high school season, I was an All-American."

Another player Robinson coached at Pershing was American Basketball Association legend Mel Daniels, five years Spencer's senior, who, in an ironic twist of fate, foreshadowed Haywood's experience entering the pro ranks. After rejecting Oscar

Robertson's Cincinnati Royals, Daniels became the first NBA first-round pick to snub the established league and go to the ABA.

Pursued by other programs—"There were 372 schools knocking down my door"—Haywood accepted a scholarship offer from Tennessee. He would have been the SEC's first Black basketball player, but legendary Kentucky head coach Adolph Rupp intervened, insisting that his program would decide when and where the league became integrated. So in 1967 Haywood went to Trinidad Junior College in Colorado, where he averaged twenty-eight points and twenty-two rebounds and earned All-American status. After one year at junior college, Haywood was chosen to play for the 1968 Olympic team, which won the gold in Mexico City. The U.S. team, led by Spencer, crushed all nine of their opponents by an average margin of twenty-seven points. "I was this nineteen-year-old kid out there. We were never supposed to win. They didn't know me. I had God on my side in the Olympics," Haywood said. "I set records for scoring, rebounding, field goal percentage, and blocked shots. 'Who is this young guy?' they asked."

And something else happened that week. This was the 1968 Olympics, famous for the iconic image of USA runners John Carlos and Tommie Smith standing on the podium, raising black-gloved fists. Few understood the message they were trying to send. They were trying to raise awareness of suffering; they were not Black Panthers or separatists. Smith and Carlos explained that they sought to make a "human rights salute," not a Black power salute.

In a 2018 *New York Times* opinion piece titled "Why Two Black Athletes Raised Their Fists during the Anthem," Avery Brundage, at the time chairman of the International Olympic Committee, a notorious racist, anti-Semite, and Nazi sympathizer, complained loudly about the "nasty demonstration against the American flag by Negroes," as if "Negroes" were not fully American. That was exactly the point Smith and Carlos were trying to make.

Haywood returned from the Olympics with a plan to play at the University of Detroit and get Coach Robinson chosen as the first Black coach in the NCAA. But once Spencer officially signed, the school reneged on their promise to hire Robinson. Spencer felt betrayed. "They decided they didn't want a Black coach," Haywood said. He wanted to leave school, but he was out of options.

So he played one season at the University of Detroit and made first team All-American, along with Kareem Abdul-Jabbar and Pete Maravich. Haywood averaged thirty-two points while leading the nation in rebounding at twenty-one boards a game, but he did not want to return without Robinson, who, after one more year at Pershing, eventually took a job at Illinois State, thus becoming the first Black NCAA basketball coach.

Haywood faced a dilemma. Transferring would mean he'd have to wait a year before playing again; he was invited to join the new professional league. "The ABA called," said Haywood. "They had missed out on Kareem. I was an underclassman and not allowed to play, but the ABA made an amendment they (ironically) called the 'reparation card,' giving me a chance to play so I could save my family."

After arguably the greatest rookie professional season ever outside of Wilt Chamberlain, with the Denver Rockets (1969–1970), one in which he averaged thirty points and nearly twenty rebounds a game, Spencer was at another crossroads. But he was "built for this," as he said. He had grown up facing down two-hundred-pound bales of cotton and racism so extreme that he had to flee his hometown. Getting paid to play a game he loved was not hard; sticking up for his rights was what separated Spencer Haywood from the others.

In his interview with the authors, Haywood recalled one of his mentors, NBA Hall of Fame player and coach Lenny Wilkens, who played a key role in Spencer's life. "Lenny was a coach and a father on the floor for me. His was like your big brother; you better listen. You gotta remember, I was twenty years old. He spent lots of time with me off the court. I remember we were in Boston once, and he said, 'I'm gonna take you to the best seafood restaurant in town.'

"So we get there and I order two filet mignons. He just looked at me and shook his head," Haywood chuckled. "After that I ordered a shrimp cocktail!"

Wilkens said about Spencer, "He's the Curt Flood of the NBA. A lot of young guys should look up to him, because he's made them a lot of money."

Spencer had five great years in Seattle. He was named to the All-NBA first team in 1972 and 1973 and the All-NBA second team in 1974 and 1975. He still holds single-season record averages for points and rebounds. Haywood played in four All-Star Games while with Seattle and led them to their first play-off berth in 1975.

In 1975, the Supersonics traded Haywood to the New York Knicks. Haywood later played for the New Orleans Jazz, the Los Angeles Lakers, and the Washington Bullets, finishing his career in 1983.

In the 1970s and 1980s, Spencer Haywood had his problems with substance abuse and addiction. He has thirty-seven years of sobriety under his belt. For years he has been traveling around the county giving talks about his experience, trying to impress upon young people the need to work hard, be serious and disciplined, and learn about history. He runs the Spencer Haywood Foundation, a nonprofit. And his advice to young basketball players who want to play at a high level?

"Go for it with all the gusto. Make sure that you love the game. If you love it, it's not work. It is joy." And when asked about athletes in the spotlight today, he said, "I like Colin Kaepernick. He paid the ultimate price. But he has been vindicated."

When Spencer was inducted into the Hall of Fame in 2015, he went in as a Sonic. But now he doesn't want to talk so much about his exploits on the court.

"The 'one and done' rule should be removed," he said. "Think about it. When Bill Gates and Steve Jobs drop out of college and make billions, nobody says, 'They should have finished college!' But when a Black player leaves early, it's like, 'Oh, wait a minute—we love this slave labor they are providing us. He's giving up an education.' These colleges are getting free labor out of basketball and football players. They bring in so much money for the schools and get nothing. Pay them!"

"When I went into the NBA Hall of Fame in 2015, I had to wait twenty-seven years after my playing days were over, just like Nelson Mandela waited in jail," Haywood said in an interview with the authors. He thought of God during the induction ceremony. "He may not come when you want him, but he's always right on time, I said that day. The other part I left out of my speech was that I would not be complete with this journey until I see Curt Flood in the Hall of Fame. I'm just saying to baseball, they need to wake the hell up.

"I was the chairman of the retired NBA players' association for years. They put me in that position because they knew I would fight for them until I die. And my term ran out some time ago; I needed a break."

"My rule is on the desk of the NBA and the players' association," Spencer said. "You'd think, wouldn't you believe in the days of Black Lives Matter, here's a Black life that created the wealth for you and your family. We gotta change the name of this rule; there's only one rule. All they have to do is make a simple change in the bylaws and call it what it really is—the Spencer Haywood Tule.

"How do you not know your history? They said I was a militant. I was just trying to get my mother out of the cotton fields. I was a twenty-year-old kid suing the NBA, and it got all the way to the Supreme Court."

Because of Spencer Haywood and Curt Flood, athletic labor is now free to seek what it couldn't half a century ago: its own place of employment for a salary determined through negotiation, just like anyone else in a free society.

About the "one-and-done" rule, Haywood said, "I own those trademarks. You can't just take Black history and throw it away. I know that the NBA is still mad about me suing them," he said. "I risked it all, and I still take abuse. They sometimes don't want me to speak at athletic departments, afraid I might rile them up, so I speak at the law schools," he laughed.

When asked about what he thinks his legacy will be, Spencer spoke directly. "I saved America's butt in the 1968 Olympics, and I saved Black athletes' butts so they could make some money. I went to the Supreme Court to change basketball and football as we know it today. And I gave them the Spencer Haywood Rule."

Spencer Haywood is not an angry man; rather, he is a proud man who just wants the proper recognition for something he did that changed the world. Nowadays, Spencer Haywood lives in Las Vegas, enjoys golf, and is a proud father of four daughters and three grandchildren. "I got a lot of gratitude. I got a wonderful family—and a great golf course near my house," he said.

"We still got to fight, [the late NBA commissioner] David Stern told me before he passed away," Spencer added. "Mr. Stern told me, 'It's been almost fifty years. I've gotta do some good before I get outta here. The first step starts with you.'"

Somewhere Curt Flood is very proud of Spencer Haywood, who took the first step and is still walking toward the light, fighting the good fight.

5

Baseball's Triple Trailblazer

Toni Stone

Toni Stone was always antsy. When she was young, she didn't like to stay in one place. Born in West Virginia and raised in Minnesota, she moved to San Francisco as a young woman, did a stint in New Orleans, and came back to the Bay Area for the remainder of her life. Toni always liked to be first. Growing up as a self-described "tomboy," she had a nervous energy, one that expressed itself through the beauty of our national pastime. Quite simply, Toni Stone was a ballplayer.

Toni Stone was not the kind of person to be intimidated, and she took life as it came, approaching each day and each new challenge with an open mind and an uncomplicated perspective. She had an uncanny ability to look at the ups and downs of life with a stoic, unflappable eye. At sixteen she worked out with AAA players and held her own. At twenty-five she was touring with a semiprofessional barnstorming men's team, and by the time she was thirty-one, she was playing second base on a bona fide professional Negro League team.

Toni Stone was baseball's "triple trailblazer" because she was a woman, she was African American, and she was able to overcome the idea that women "did not play baseball." She overcame all of those barriers and then some and thrived. Hers was a full life, and one that needs to be honored.

There have been few people in the arc of American sports who have made a historical impact in more than one arena, let alone three. All the men in this book, for example, had to fight to overcome the indignities and pain of prejudice, bigotry, discrimination, xenophobia, and intolerance to achieve greatness in their chosen field.

Toni Stone. Baseball's triple trailblazer, on deck to eternity.
Courtesy of the Negro Leagues Baseball Museum, Inc.

Not only did Toni Stone have to overcome all of those, but she also had to deal with two more things: the immovable forces of sexism and male chauvinism, which for a young woman growing up in the 1920s and 1930s must have been nearly as onerous as the sting of racism, and also the deep-seated notion that *girls can't play baseball.* Hers was not a Hollywood experience like the glamorous Geena Davis's portrayal of Dottie Hinson in the acclaimed 1992 film *A League of Their Own.* For Marcenia Lyle "Toni" Stone, the first woman to play organized professional baseball, it was real life—and it was her life.

Toni Stone was born in 1921, one year after the creation of the Negro Leagues, in Bluefield, West Virginia, a small city at the far southern end of the state, close to

Virginia. To put this time and place into a historical framework, the second wave of the Ku Klux Klan began during World War I and flourished in the early to mid-1920s. Feeding off the xenophobic, anti-Semitic, anti-Catholic, racist, and nationalist sentiment that was heightened during the war years, the KKK promoted itself as a "100 percent American organization."

It spread its membership and white supremacist message of hate across the country, including West Virginia. As the African American population of the state increased, so did racial hostility. In 1919, a white mob lynched two Black coal miners, and by the next year, chapters of the Klan began to emerge throughout the state. In 1922, Governor Ephraim Morgan denied a plea for clemency and permitted a Black man, Leroy Williams, to hang for the rape of a white woman, despite evidence suggesting his innocence.

In 1930, in Gauley Bridge, fifty miles north of Bluefield, the Hawks Nest Tunnel disaster claimed the lives of hundreds of workers, killed by silicosis caused by their exposure to silica dust while working in the tunnel. A majority of them were African Americans who had traveled from the South for the work. Some of the dead were buried in a mass grave nearby to hide the actual number of casualties, which may have been even more than the stated number of 764. It was the worst industrial disaster in U.S. history.

On December 10, 1931, two Black men accused of killing two white constables were forcibly removed from the Greenbrier County Jail in Lewisburg by a mob of about sixty men and lynched, their bodies riddled with bullets.

And that was the winter that Marcenia Stone's parents left Bluefield for St. Paul, Minnesota.

Her mother, Willa, was a beautician, and her father, Boykin, was a barber. She was ten years old when they moved. Marcenia was always different: extroverted, physical, stubborn, and fiercely independent. Hers was a happy, modest, hardworking family, and they were glad to get away from the provincial, narrow, and often racist culture of Bluefield. She eventually adopted the name Toni because she had been called "Tomboy" as a girl, and Toni sounded like "Tomboy."

In a 1996 interview with Merlene Davis of the *Lexington Herald-Leader*, Stone said, "I loved my trousers, my jeans. I loved cars. Most of all I loved to ride horses with no saddles. I wasn't classified. People weren't ready for me." In the 1930s, a girl who wanted to play baseball was considered a disgrace to society. Her parents' futile arguments against sports, specifically baseball, had no effect, and they supported her nonetheless. She developed a love for other sports including track and ice skating, but baseball was the one for her. Despite obvious obstacles, Stone was determined to play.

Her first year in St. Paul, she played on a team sponsored by Wheaties cereal for youngsters who had collected enough box tops. It was the Catholic Midget League, comparable to today's Little League. She went on to play for the Girls' Highlex Softball Club. A fast, strong, outstanding athlete who excelled at a variety of sports, Stone turned heads in the school and citywide sports leagues.

By the time she was fifteen, she had lettered in tennis, track, and softball for Hammond Junior High School. She also achieved honors from the citywide Junior High School Girls' Athletic Association and became the first girl to earn three separate letters in one year. Stone enrolled at Roosevelt High School, across the Mississippi River in Minneapolis.

"We do not hesitate," the *Minneapolis Star* gushed about her in 1937, "to predict that someday she will acquire the fame of Babe Didrikson." Mildred "Babe" Didrikson, from Port Arthur, Texas, for decades was considered the finest all-around woman athlete of the twentieth century, excelling in track, golf, softball, basketball, and other sports. "I could outscore and outhit her," Toni said years later in the 2010 book *Curveball: The Remarkable Story of Toni Stone, the First Woman to Play Professional Baseball in the Negro League* by Martha Ackmann. Despite her success in sports, Toni was bored in the classroom and often cut school, dropping out after her first year when she was fifteen.

She joined a local American Legion championship team and played second base with the Twin Cities Colored Giants semipro team, a local barnstorming club that traveled around the Midwest and Canada. During their 1937 season, Stone worked out with the newly formed St. Paul Saints of the American Association, the AAA affiliate of the Chicago White Sox. To work out with players who were just one step away from "the show" must have been quite a thrill for the sixteen-year-old local girl.

That fall she moved to the San Francisco Bay Area to care for her sick sister Bunny. Friends and relatives said that they knew she'd eventually leave St. Paul, probably for a place that had more excitement and appeal. During and after the war, the San Francisco Bay Area was exploding, economically, culturally, and socially. The shipyards had brought thousands of African Americans from the South for jobs, and the war had brought thousands of soldiers returning from the war in the Pacific, many of whom decided to settle there.

She fell in love with what she called "My San Francisco." She worked at a shipyard in the daytime as a forklift operator, and at night in a cafeteria. And she hardly played baseball at all. But in 1946, at the age of twenty-five, Stone returned to the game she loved, joining up with a barnstorming semipro team, the San Francisco Sea Lions. In her first at bat, she drove in two runs and from then on was accepted by most of the players.

Stone married San Francisco native and former military man Aurelious Alberga in 1950, a man thirty-seven years her senior whom she met in a San Francisco nightclub. He did not approve of her playing baseball but went along with it begrudgingly for the next four years.

They stayed together until his death in 1987 at 103. Alberga served in World War I and graduated from officer candidate school after the war in 1919, becoming one of the army's first Black commissioned officers. Later in his military career, he served as an infantry instruction officer. After leaving the army, Alberga worked for a bail bond company, retiring in the 1960s. He also organized several drum and bugle corps in the Bay Area.

After a dispute about pay that she had been promised by the Sea Lions, Stone quit the team and joined the Black Pelicans, New Orleans' original baseball team, which lasted from its inception in 1887 to 1959. The Pelicans, whose name is currently carried by the local NBA team, were the prime factor in weaving baseball into the fabric of New Orleans as a family, neighborhood experience long before television, fancy stadiums, and corporate skyboxes changed the face of professional sports.

After a short stint with that team, she joined the New Orleans Creoles. Black baseball enthusiasts and local businessmen had created both teams as members of the Negro Southern League. Though these teams were primarily composed of men, the New Orleans Creoles began hiring women in the 1940s. Stone stayed with them until 1952. Her husband was still not keen on her baseball career, but during the spring and summer she continued traveling the country playing ball and then returning home to what became their home in Oakland in the off-season.

In early 1953, Toni, now thirty-one, was signed by Syd Pollack, owner of the Indianapolis Clowns of the Negro Leagues, to play second base; Hank Aaron had played second base and shortstop for the team one year earlier before getting signed and fast-tracked through the minors by the Milwaukee Braves.

Pollack did this as part of a publicity stunt. The Clowns, fitting for their name, were compared to the Harlem Globetrotters of the basketball world; having a woman on the team attracted more fans. But Toni was not a clown; she was a ballplayer. Over the fifty games Stone appeared in for the Clowns that year, she had a .243 batting average, with above-average speed, and showed a good glove at second base.

Stone was the first woman in the organized Negro Leagues and, as such, drew a great deal of attention. Some had to do with her baseball skills, but much of it focused on her feminine side. A set of pictures—one showing her in a dress getting out of a car and another in her Clowns uniform getting off the team bus—in the July 1953 issue of *Ebony* was accompanied by the caption, "Dressed in street clothes, Toni Stone is an attractive young lady who could be someone's secretary, but once in uniform she is all ballplayer."

What *Ebony* apparently didn't want to mention was that there were constant instances of racial and sexual segregation that often presented hardship. Hotels that booked Black Americans did not allow a woman to be roommates with a man, so Stone was often forced to bunk in a house of prostitution.

And when buses stopped for bathroom breaks, her teammates would urinate using the bus as cover. She had to find a more private spot, often in the dark of night. The article included an explanation from Stone of how she deftly handled herself amid a group of men, only some of which was printed in the magazine.

The *Ebony* article wrote at the time, "While most sports fans were sure that the Clowns signed Toni merely as an extra box-office attraction—the team features baseball comedy and 'Spike-Jones like' music on its barnstorming tours—the young lady has surprised everybody by turning in a businesslike job at both second base and at the plate. In her first game she walked and then drove in two runs with a sharp single."

"At first, the fellows made passes at me, but my situation traveling around the country with a busload of guys wasn't any different from that of the girl singers who travel with jazz bands," she said, "and once you let the guys know that there isn't going to be any monkey business, they give you their respect. They didn't mean any harm, and in their way they liked me. Just that I wasn't supposed to be there. They'd tell me to 'go home and fix my husband some biscuits or any damn thing. Just get the hell away from here.'"

All information about Stone listed her age as twenty-two, nine years younger than she really was, although she did look younger. Part of the campaign to promote Stone included exaggeration of her schooling, claiming she had a master's degree when, in reality, she did not even graduate from high school back in St. Paul.

In the games she did play—50 out of the 175 the Clowns played that year—she normally came out by the middle innings, giving her a chance to shower and change back into her street clothes before the rest of the team came in. Stone would get dressed in the umpires' room.

Once again, there was never any consideration or attempt to make her life easier. The innumerable hardships she had to endure as a Black female ballplayer were ignored by the team, which was a microcosm of society.

After the 1953 season, Stone's contract was sold to the Kansas City Monarchs. In 1945, UCLA football star and army lieutenant Jackie Robinson, then twenty-five, hit .387 as the Monarchs' shortstop, thus becoming the first Monarch to make the jump from the Negro Leagues to Major League Baseball, signing with the Brooklyn Dodgers in 1946. While playing for the Monarchs, who were managed by Negro League legend and future Hall of Famer Buck O'Neil, Toni spent most of the game on the bench, next to men who for the most part resented her.

"It was hell," she said. At Kansas City she hardly got any playing time. Her spot in the Clowns' infield was taken by a woman, Connie Morgan, and the Clowns added another woman, pitcher Mamie "Peanut" Johnson. Following the 1954 season, Stone retired from professional baseball, but she continued to play amateur baseball for many years. Shortly after that, Stone moved back to Oakland to work as a nurse and care for her sick husband.

In 1990, she was included in two exhibits at the Baseball Hall of Fame, one on "Women in Baseball" and another on Negro League baseball. In 1990, Stone's hometown of St. Paul declared March 6 "Toni Stone Day." And in 1993, Stone was inducted into the Women's Sports Hall of Fame. St. Paul also has a baseball field named after her.

In her profile of Negro League female ballplayers in the October 13, 2020, issue of *Sports Illustrated*, Holly Van Leuven wrote that Stone recalled being shunned by teammates. But she also remembered kinder teammates in whom she could confide. "A woman has her dreams, too," she told one. "When you finish high school, they tell a boy to go out and see the world. What do they tell a girl? They tell her to go next door and marry the boy that their families picked for her. It wasn't right. A woman can do many things."

Hall of Famer Toni Stone, a true triple trailblazer, died on November 2, 1996, at a nursing home in Alameda, California. She was seventy-five years old. And in 2000, in Oakland, California, Toni Stone was inducted posthumously into the very first class of the African American Ethnic Sports Hall of Fame as part of the inaugural ceremony.

Toni Stone has largely been relegated to a footnote in history, one in a long list of African American women who endured hardships, overcame discrimination, and helped shape the nation, only to be shoved aside, their contributions minimized. But fittingly, on the first day of summer, June 20, 2019, the Roundabout Theatre Company production of Lydia R. Diamond's play *Toni Stone* officially opened to terrific reviews off-Broadway in New York.

The moving drama, which featured a cast of nine—one woman and eight men in multiple roles—succeeds in correcting the injustice that Stone was perhaps not as culturally important as Jackie Robinson or Satchel Paige. *Toni Stone*, based on Ackmann's book, was scheduled to open May 2, 2020, at the ACT Theater in San Francisco but was indefinitely postponed due to the coronavirus.

The following is Jesse Green's June 20, 2019, *New York Times* review of the Roundabout Theater production:

"Stone in 1953 became the first woman of any race to play in a pro baseball game, and was obsessed since childhood with the sport. This play considers her character in the context of social change reshaping the field and the country. Stone's personality remains something of a puzzle. She preferred words that approach the irreducible facticity of her beloved baseball statistics.

"In this fine play Stone, as a woman in sports, is doubly targeted, even by her own teammates. As they mistakenly mock what they assume is her lesbianism, some also threaten her sexually. But the play does not let these hostile interactions become the whole picture; sometimes Toni simply laughs them off. This is not to diminish the virulence of sexism and racism but to honor Black men and women who through sheer force of will were able to preserve meaningful lives beyond it."

Toni Stone said that her most memorable baseball moment came when she batted against the legendary Satchel Paige in a barnstorming game in 1953, when he played for the St. Louis Browns (it would be their final year; they became the Baltimore Orioles in 1954).

"He was so good," she remembered, "that he'd ask batters where they wanted it, just so they'd have a chance. He'd ask, 'You want it high? You want it low? You want it right in the middle? Just say.' People still couldn't get a hit against him. So I get up there and he says, 'Hey, T, how do you like it?' And I said, 'It doesn't matter—just don't hurt me.' When he wound up, he had these big old feet—all you could see was his shoe.

"I stood there shaking, but I got a hit—a fastball over his head into centerfield. That was the finest thing to happen to me in my life," she said. "And I was so tickled to death I was laughing all the way to first base, and started to round first base and fell. Ooh, I looked clumsy. Didn't look like no pro. I laughed like hell, and Satchel was laughing, too. Happiest moment of my life."

In 2022, five new street designs were announced to enhance the area next to Oracle Park, where the San Francisco Giants play. One will be a sculpture of Toni Stone. "Toni Stone was the first to play with and get paid by the Negro Leagues as a Black woman," said sculptor Dana King in the San Francisco website Hoodline.com, "and the jersey she wears is the one she wore playing for her first professional team, the San Francisco Sea Lions. Her number is on the back. She wears the uniform with pride, and even in its bulkiness, one senses the difference in her form, but not in her heart. Baseball is the love of her life."

Toni Stone, the triple trailblazer, enjoyed life to the fullest.

6

An American Dreamer Dives to Glory

Dr. Sammy Lee

We are living in an era where it is dangerous to be an immigrant in America. Think about that for a minute. With the exception of Native Americans, aren't we all immigrants, even those of us who arrived in chains? What happened to Emma Lazarus's words that are inscribed on the Statue of Liberty?

Give me your tired, your poor,
Your huddled masses yearning to breathe free,
The wretched refuse of your teeming shore.

What has not happened yet, tragically, is our will as a nation to get beyond prejudice, to heal from the affliction of racism. "I look to a day when people will not be judged by the color of their skin, but by the content of their character," said Martin Luther King Jr., who was vilified and accused of being a communist. Now he is venerated, his name on schools and great boulevards across this country. But the work is not done; in fact, as evidenced by recent history, it is just beginning.

Dr. Sammy Lee was a first-generation American, the product of an arranged marriage. His parents arrived in 1905, right in the middle of the Great Immigration. But they were not from Europe like over 90 percent of their fellow newcomers; they were from Korea, and their son, blessed with a determination and fierce work ethic, grew up to be the greatest in the world at his chosen sport, a fun activity we all do as kids in between swimming pool games of Marco Polo—diving. Olympic gold medalist Dr. Sammy Lee dove into the pool of glory and came up a champion.

Asian immigrants began to arrive in this country in 1850. The first wave came from China, single men who worked for a while and returned home. At first they were attracted by the gold rush in California. Many prospected for gold on their

Sammy Lee. Patriotism personified.
African American Ethnic Sports Hall of Fame

own or labored for other miners. Soon many opened businesses such as restaurants and laundries. After the gold rush, Chinese worked as agricultural laborers, and by the 1860s, thousands had sailed across the ocean to work on the transcontinental railroad, which would connect the Union Pacific and the Central Pacific lines in Promontory, Utah, in 1867, thus opening up unlimited economic possibilities for the young country just two years after the horrible, bloody Civil War.

But with the onset of hard economic times in the 1870s, other immigrants began to compete for jobs traditionally reserved for the Chinese. And with economic competition came racial suspicion, hatred, and anti-Chinese riots, especially in California. The Chinese Exclusion Act of 1882, prohibiting all immigration of Chinese laborers, revealed the depth of the racist hypocrisy of our government's misguided policy. In 1924 the U.S. Congress designated Asia as a "barred zone" from which immigration was totally prohibited. These acts were in place until 1952, when the Immigration Act abolished racial barriers.

But it was not only the Chinese who emigrated from Asia. In the decades before World War II, thousands of Japanese came to California and built productive communities throughout the state, based mainly on agriculture and other small businesses, with a tremendous emphasis on education. But the war brought the ugliness and horror of the internment camps, rupturing the Japanese community. Their resilience was tested, and after the war, the Japanese American community emerged stronger than ever.

Less is known about the story of Korean Americans in this country. The first wave of Korean immigration to the United States, from 1903 to 1905, consisted of about seven thousand young men, mostly Christians, who went to work on Hawaii's sugar plantations as contract laborers. Of those, about two thousand migrated to the mainland. Most of these immigrants settled in California and dispersed all over the state, both north and south and in the valleys, as farmworkers or laborers in mines and on the railroads.

Despite having to deal with the same systemic racism that the Chinese and Japanese had faced, which made it difficult and challenging to achieve their piece of the American dream, the Korean community in America has expanded and thrived, a tribute to their work ethic and perseverance. Today there are approximately 1.7 million Korean Americans, 90 percent of whom reside in California.

Dr. Samuel "Sammy" Lee was born Samuel Rhee in 1920, the youngest of five children of immigrant parents who married in Korea, fulfilling an arrangement by their respective families. They moved to California in 1905 and settled in Fresno, where they changed their name to Lee. His father graduated with a degree in civil engineering from Occidental College, but, unable to find work due to his Asian ancestry, he was forced to open a restaurant and market.

His parents sacrificed greatly for their youngest son and had hopes that Sammy would be their realization of the American dream. As a teenager in the 1930s living in Pasadena, he would go to the Brookside Park Plunge swimming pool but was able to swim only on Wednesdays, the one day of the week the pool was not segregated.

"Basically, anyone who wasn't white could use the pool," said Paula K. Yoo, author of the book *Sixteen Years in Sixteen Seconds*. "Then they'd drain it afterward."

So when Sammy was told that he couldn't use the pool except for that day, he was not to be denied. He found a coach who had him dive over a sand pit because it had one advantage over water: it gave him stronger leg muscles, which is why he was able to jump high and perform beautifully executed triple-somersault dives. Sammy was valedictorian of both his junior high and high school graduating classes and was named best athlete at the latter. He developed a passion for swimming and diving and was dedicated to practicing long and hard. It was also his way of addressing the problem of segregation and racism.

After showing great promise as a diver, Lee decided to pursue his dream of becoming an Olympian and dedicated himself to his passion. He went to his father's alma mater, Occidental College in Los Angeles, and while there he won the 1942 national AAU championships in both the 3-meter springboard and 10-meter platform events. Lee utilized his short stature in his dives, tucking tighter and turning faster than his opponents.

At Occidental he majored in premed, studying long hours to become a doctor, but he managed to find time for diving. He spent hours in labs and then practiced diving to unwind. The diminutive Sammy, who stood only 5'1", had two lofty goals: to be an Olympic champion and a medical doctor. He had promised his father that he would do both.

After graduating from Occidental in 1943, Lee entered the University of Southern California Medical School and briefly retired from diving. However, he returned to competition in 1946 and again won the national AAU championship in the platform event. He received his MD in 1947. All the practicing and dedication paid off for Sammy when he made the U.S. Olympic team. The Games had been postponed twice because of the war and finally took place in 1948 in London.

He became the first Asian American to win an Olympic gold medal for the United States and the first man to win back-to-back gold medals in Olympic platform diving, winning consecutive championships at the 1948 Games and again in 1952 at the Helsinki Games. He also won a bronze medal in springboard diving at the 1948 Games. Lee is a member of the International Swimming Hall of Fame and the U.S. Olympic Hall of Fame.

On July 26, 1948, President Harry Truman issued Executive Order 9981, ending segregation in the military. Ten days later, Sammy won his first Olympic gold medal. In 1952, four years after his Olympic triumph in London, Dr. Lee enthusiastically embraced Truman's historic order and joined the U.S. Army Medical Corps, achieving the rank of major. He fully expected to serve in the Korean War but instead was sent to compete in the Olympic Games, taking the gold in the 10-meter platform competition at Helsinki and becoming the only Asian American to win two consecutive Olympic gold medals.

The war ended in 1953, and Dr. Sammy Lee went on to serve in South Korea from 1953 to 1955, where he specialized in diseases of the ear. In 1953, while in Korea, he won the James E. Sullivan Award in 1953, awarded annually by the Amateur Athletic Union to the most outstanding amateur athlete in the United States.

But, like other minority Olympians, his gold medals and military service didn't help him back home. The difficulty he and his wife Rosalind experienced when they tried to purchase a home in Orange County became a national news story—and a scandal.

His athletic and patriotic achievements did not spare him and Rosalind from discrimination when he tried to buy a home in Garden Grove, California, a booming community where he wanted to open a medical practice. In Yoo's book, she relates the story of his difficulties—as an Olympic champion—finding a place to live. When turning him away, real estate agents were candid. "I'm sorry, Doctor," he remembered one telling him, "but I have to eat, and I'd lose my job for selling to a nonwhite."

Eventually they were able to purchase a home from a developer who appreciated Sammy's devotion to his country, and his winning two gold medals.

Wyomia Tyus was the first person to win consecutive gold medals in the 100 meters, at Tokyo in 1964 and Mexico City in 1968. She also won a gold medal in the 400-meter relay at Mexico City and a silver medal in the same event at the 1964 Tokyo Games. She knew Sammy from their shared Olympic experiences.

"I knew Dr. Sammy Lee as an incredible Olympic gold medal diver. I really got to know him when we were both chosen to bring in the Olympic flag at the 1984 Games. He was an incredible joke teller and kept everyone he met entertained," Tyus said in an interview with the authors.

He went on to serve on the President's Council for Physical Fitness over five administrations and as a goodwill ambassador to Asia. Later, he spoke of those tours on behalf of the State Department. "Whenever I was asked by those people in the Far East how America treated Oriental people, I told them the truth," he recalled on the website www.thesammyleestory.com. "I said Americans had their shortcomings, but they had guts enough to advertise them, whereas others try to cover them up."

Dr. Lee had stellar careers in both coaching and diving. He served as coach of the 1960 U.S. Olympic diving team and also of the 1964 Japanese and Korean teams. He coached everyone from students in the family pool to Olympic divers, including four-time gold medalist Pat McCormick and two-time gold medalist Bob Webster.

Dr. Lee was the proud mentor to four-time Olympic gold medalist Greg Louganis, the second diver in history to sweep the diving events in consecutive Olympic Games. Louganis has been described as the greatest American diver, and by some as the greatest diver in history.

Sammy Lee became a very successful physician and practiced for thirty-seven years as an ear, nose, and throat doctor before retiring in 1990. He would go swimming in his community several times a week. And the pool that barred him as a child changed their policy after he returned home with the gold medal.

That pool is now named after him, as well as the Dr. Sammy Lee Medical and Health Science Magnet Elementary School in LA, which serves a diverse student body. In 2018, the school received a California Distinguished School Award.

"I was pleased and honored to induct Sammy in 2013 to the African American Ethnic Sports Hall of Fame in Koreatown in Los Angeles, and while there I visited the elementary school named after him and attended the naming of Dr. Sammy Lee Square in Koreatown by the City of Los Angeles," said Arif Khatib. "When I inducted Sammy, there was an overflow crowd in attendance to support him.

"At the induction ceremony, he shared with me some of his Olympic experiences; he spoke of spending countless hours in isolation from the white swimmers. On the day he was inducted, Wyomia Tyus remarked, 'Dr. Sammy was an outstanding family man, athlete, a great coach, a fantastic doctor, and friend to many. This is why I nominated him to be inducted into this hall of fame. He is missed very much by me and the many others whose lives he touched.'"

Khatib added an anecdote about Sammy. "Sammy was a gentleman at all times, and his wife Rosalind said that was one of the reasons she was attracted to him. He lived in Orange County, and when he arrived at the downtown hotel in his Mercedes, I noticed he was driving, and his wife was his passenger. He was ninety at the time. Upon his arrival, I asked him, 'Sammy, why didn't your daughter drive you?' He said, 'I'd rather drive myself.'

"Later, when he began to experience early dementia, he would still go to the neighborhood pool and swim. On one of those trips he became lost. His wife phoned me and said, 'Arif, they can't find Sammy. He left for the pool and didn't return.' I assured her they would find him and asked her to let me know when they did. Later I received the call that the police had finally found him and brought him home. He called to tell me they had taken his driver's license and he could not drive anymore. I understood and said I would stay in touch on a regular basis.

"He and I stayed in touch until his death, and we spoke on a regular basis about sports in general and swimming in particular. Dr. Sammy Lee was a family man, a patriot, a physician, a coach, and an Olympic champion."

In a 2006 interview with the *Orange County Register*, Sammy said, "Prejudice made me more determined to succeed in the American way of life. I wanted to represent the finest qualities of my ancestral background and show that they can be accepted as 100 percent American. I tell the kids today that if you've got the fighting instinct in you, you can overcome prejudice. You show people with your performance, not just words."

When Sammy Lee passed away in 2016 at the age of ninety-six, he left an amazing legacy of athletic achievement, service to his country, a lifetime of commitment to medicine, and perseverance. His son Sammy II said this about this father: "He didn't care about anyone's race, religion, ethnicity, or sexual preference, and if you look at his divers, it was really a multination of people he helped."

7

His Best Was Sure Good Enough

Burl Toler

It was a warm September night in 2000, and standing on the sidelines, pen and legal pad in hand, was a reporter waiting for the kickoff of the opening football game of the season at Encinal High School in Alameda, California.

The whistle blew, and within seconds a kid was sprinting down the sideline, his teammates exhorting him to "take it to the house!" In pursuit were two opponents who aggressively brought him down after a long return. Tempers flared, and for a few seconds it looked like all that youthful adrenaline might result in a fight, on the very first play of the season.

But what the writer noticed was the tall older man with the white hat trailing the play. It was the referee, who somehow had been keeping up with these swift teenagers. As the players unpacked from the pile and faced off, yelling at each other like the Jets and the Sharks, the tall man waded in and effortlessly took charge, defusing the situation, separating kids while at the same time complimenting them, "Good play! Clean tackle! Okay, son, that's all right, give me the ball."

For the rest of the game, the journalist marveled at how efficient, nurturing, and respectful of the kids and coaches the older gentleman was. Afterward, he asked the side judge who the man with the white hat was. "Oh, that's Mr. Toler," he smiled, surprised that the writer didn't know who the referee was. He soon found out.

"The supreme triumph of the undefeated 1951 University of San Francisco Dons came in choosing not to accept an invitation to the Orange Bowl game under the condition that the team play without two of its best players, African Americans Ollie Matson and Burl Toler. The team's dramatic stand against racism is perhaps the single greatest symbolic victory in the history of college football."

Burl Toler. The first with the whistle.
African American Ethnic Sports Hall of Fame

That was from a University of San Francisco press release on April 7, 2017, the day Phelan Hall was renamed Burl Toler Hall. It was not the only time Burl Toler would stand at the forefront of social justice—and social change—in sports.

In *Sports Illustrated's* July 12, 1965, "For the Record" section, it read, "Appointed by the NFL as a head linesman, Burl Toler, a former University of San Francisco football star, will be the first Negro ever to serve as a field official for a major professional athletic league in the USA."

Burl Toler Sr., 1928–2009, wore many hats—not just the white hat of a referee. He was an All-American athlete, a teacher, a principal, a coach, the first African American field official to appear in any major professional American sport, an administrator, and a police commissioner, among other things.

He was a man of principle, a beacon of truth and honesty, a pillar of the community, a compassionate man who never complained about any of the barriers he had to overcome to make his way—and his mark—in the world. He was also a son, a brother, a husband, a father of six, and a grandfather of ten. And he left a tremendous legacy.

Burl Abron Toler was born in Memphis on May 9, 1928. His father, Arnold, was a Pullman porter. His mother, Annie, operated a small store and ran a boarding house. Growing up, Burl's parents stressed education. Burl went to a segregated high school but did not play football because of a severe burn on his arm incurred in an accident with a vat of cooking grease.

After graduation, he briefly attended LeMoyne College in Memphis, a historically Black college. After a year at Lemoyne, Burl moved to the Bay Area at the suggestion of his Uncle Louis, a local entrepreneur who lived in Oakland, and enrolled at the City College of San Francisco.

Noticing his size and believing Burl to be a football player, a student saw him in the hall and said, "Aren't you going to practice?" Later, an assistant coach spotted him in the gym and asked him to come out for the team. In his first practice, he tackled the star running back, Ollie Matson, on three consecutive plays. "They were like, 'Who is this guy?'" said Susan Toler Carr, Burl's daughter, in a 2020 phone interview. "After a few tackles, that's how they met. 'Hi, I'm Ollie,' and, 'I'm Burl,' and they became best friends from there."

Their 1948 team went 12-0, winning the mythical National Junior College Championship. Playing center and linebacker, Burl became a junior college All-American, and both Toler and Matson earned scholarships to the nearby University of San Francisco. For a young man who had only played organized football for a year, Burl caught on quickly.

Starters played both ways back then; Burl was a ferocious, hard-hitting linebacker with great speed on defense, and when the Dons had the ball, he played both center and receiver. His coach was a fiery young man from Notre Dame, Joe Kuharich, who had played in the NFL as an undersized guard. In 1949, they went 7-3, mostly on the strength of Toler and Matson; Burl received All-American honorable mention and All-Coast League honors.

The Dons were expected to make national noise in 1950, but though they won all seven of their home games, they went a disappointing 0-4 in road games, the worst loss coming on a 55–7 blowout at the hands of Stanford. Kuharich vowed they would be better next year—he just didn't know how much better.

In 1951, USF was known for basketball. Their team had won the National Invitational Tournament in Madison Square Garden in 1949; the historic Bill Russell/K. C. Jones NCAA championship teams would come along in 1955 and 1956. Football at USF, however, had long been an afterthought, and in 1951 the program was in financial difficulty, losing $70,000 a year, and attendance at Kezar Stadium had declined by 80 percent since the arrival of the pro team, the 49ers, in 1946. The problem was not so much winning games as getting people to watch them.

Kuharich was a fanatic about conditioning and fundamentals. His nickname was "the Barracuda," and he drove the players mercilessly. Kuharich knew he had the players to post a winning season, but he was convinced they could be a *great* team.

Gino Marchetti had quit high school his senior year to join the army and saw action in the Battle of the Bulge. Marchetti's dominance in college and then as a pass-rushing end from 1953 to 1966 for the Baltimore Colts was such that legendary coach Sid Gillman said this about him in the 1999 *Sporting News* 50 Greatest Players of All Time: "The greatest player in football. It's a waste of time to run around this guy's end. Don't bother to even try it."

Local boy Bob St. Clair entered Poly High as a 5'9", 160-pound freshman. By his senior year he was a 6'5", 215-pound two-way lineman; his teammates called him Geek. He kept growing, and by the time he got to the NFL he was 6'9", 265 pounds.

Speedster Matson had moved to San Francisco from Texas with his mother, who had made up her mind that her son should become a dentist. But Ollie had his own ambition: "I wanted to be the best football player who ever lived," he said. In 1951, Matson's senior year, he led the nation in rushing yardage and touchdowns and was selected as an All-American.

Prior to joining the NFL, Matson was part of the U.S. Olympic Team in the 1952 Games at Helsinki, Finland, winning a bronze medal in the 400-meter run and a silver in the 4×400-meter relay. From 1952 to 1966, he played for four NFL teams, earning first team all-pro honors seven times. "They'd double team him if he were sitting up in the grandstand eating hot dogs, just to make sure," said Coach Frank "Pop" Ivy to sportswriter Cooper Rollow, quoted in *Pro Football 1958*.

At USF, what Matson was to the Dons' offense, the 6'2", 210-pound Toler was to the defense. "I felt Burl was the best player of any of us," Marchetti said in a telephone interview with the *New York Times* after Toler passed away in 2009. "He was the best tackler, the hardest hitter, and besides Ollie had the most speed."

Their offense put up an average of thirty-one points per game in the 1951 season, while holding their opponents to just eight points a contest. They went 9-0, their big win a payback victory in New York City versus eastern powerhouse Fordham.

In early December, Kuharich got a letter from the Orange Bowl committee that read, "You are invited to play in the Orange Bowl—but you must leave the two Black players at home." He read it to his players, who were assembled in the team room. The players did not mince words with their response.

In the 2016 piece, "1951 USF Dons: The Team That Stood Tall," NFL.com news quoted Bill Henneberry, who was the Dons' backup quarterback at the time: "We told them to go to hell. If Ollie and Burl didn't go, none of us were going. We walked out, and that was the end of it."

At that time the major bowls, all except the Rose and the Sun, would only invite southeastern teams. USF had defeated the College of the Pacific 47–14 in a game that was supposed to determine which team went to a bowl. Instead, Pacific went to the Sun Bowl, and the Dons got nothing. In the same article, Henneberry was not the only Don who had something to say decades later about the incident.

"When we found out Burl and Ollie weren't going to go, we said, 'Stick it in your butt—we ain't going,'" Marchetti said. "But you never heard anybody on the team squawk about it." "What we should've done," joked halfback/safety Joe Scudero, "was to send Ollie and Burl to one of those bowls and leave the rest of us home. Hell, the two of them could've beaten those Southern schools by themselves."

The announced reason for rejecting USF for a bowl game was its soft schedule. But it came out later that the Gator, Sugar, and Orange Bowl committees had decided to avoid teams with Black players. "We were disappointed at the time, sure," Burl Toler, gracious as always, told the *San Francisco Chronicle* in a 2001 interview on the fiftieth anniversary of that historic season. "But it was not what the team, our coach or the university stood for. We were very fortunate and blessed to have had a group like that."

Nine of the Dons were drafted by the NFL. Matson, Marchetti, and St. Clair were inducted into the Hall of Fame, the most ever from a single college team. That brave decision cost the school $100,000 and was the death knell for football at USF. Kuharich resigned to accept a coaching job with the NFL Chicago Cardinals. On December 30, 1951, the school disbanded the program; their best football team was to be its last for a while. USF football returned in the 1960s but was dropped again after the 1982 season, this time forever.

In 2000, the U.S. Senate unanimously passed a resolution, submitted by Barbara Boxer of California, acknowledging that the Dons were victimized by racial prejudice, that the treatment they endured was wrong, and that recognition for their accomplishments was overdue.

Burl graduated with a degree in education in 1952 and in June was drafted by the Cleveland Browns. He also got married that year to his wife Melvia, and the two were together for thirty-nine years. In July he was traded to the Chicago Cardinals before training camp started. He seemed to be on his way.

Matson, Marchetti, and Toler were invited to play in the 1952 College All-Star Game against the NFL champion Los Angeles Rams, one of the greatest teams ever assembled, with five future Hall of Famers. The Rams were also the first team in the modern NFL to sign Black players, who were an integral part of the team that won the first-ever major sports championship on the West Coast.

More than eighty-eight thousand fans packed Chicago's Soldier Field on a rainy Friday night in August 1952. The college stars outplayed the Rams but lost, 10–7. Toler, playing out of position at defensive end, was on his way to becoming the game MVP when, in the fourth quarter, while wiping out three Ram offensive lineman, his right knee was shattered by a blindside block. He never totally healed and would not play a down in the NFL.

"I had planned to play professional football, but I was also always interested in education," Toler said in a 1968 interview, reprinted in *Profiles, Football Zebras* in a piece by Mark Schulz. "The knee injury led me into education sooner."

Burl Toler loved San Francisco and remained in the city after graduating from USF, and he obtained teaching credentials during this time. He took a job teaching math and PE at Benjamin Franklin Middle School in San Francisco. For seventeen years at Franklin, he also coached sports and worked as a counselor.

Toler was a natural, a calm, consistent, and fair presence in the classroom who loved teaching and being around children, and in 1968, when he was forty, he became the first African American secondary school principal in the district. Altogether he spent twenty-five years in the SF school district. Franklin School closed in 2004 but reopened two years later when the city council honored Toler in 2006 by renaming the school Burl A. Toler Middle School.

In 1966, Burl returned to USF where he earned a master's degree in educational administration. After his stint as principal, Toler served as a commissioner of the San Francisco Police Department from 1978 to 1986. He was honored in 2009 by the police commission; this is an excerpt from that ceremony:

"This is a presentation of a certificate of merit and appreciation to the family of former police commissioner Burl A. Toler. Even with being part of the city, he loved San Francisco and what the city stood for. It is a privilege to honor him in this forum not just for his work as commissioner but for discharging his duties with integrity, courage, and professionalism."

Burl served on the board of trustees of USF from 1987 until 1998. From 1971 to 1991, he was director of personnel for the Centers Division of the San Francisco Community College District, where he was responsible for 1,100 teachers and administrators.

In 1965, former USF sports information director, NFL commissioner Pete Rozelle, asked his old USF friend Burl Toler to become the league's first Black official. Thus he became the first African American to serve as a field official in a major American professional sports league. Burl Toler would spend twenty-five years as a league official.

He was appointed as a head linesman prior to the 1965 season, and in 1980 he was the first African American official to work a Super Bowl. Toler also worked the 1982 AFC championship game between the San Diego Chargers and Cincinnati Bengals at Cincinnati's Riverfront Stadium, possibly the coldest game in NFL history. The air temperature was minus nine degrees, but the wind chill was minus fifty-nine. The game would later become known as the "Freezer Bowl."

Once, at a game in Milwaukee, Gino Marchetti rushed up to rookie line judge Toler and held him in a warm embrace. Toler was touched by the gesture but was at the same time conscious of a possible breach in decorum. "Gino," he protested, "you can't do this!"

From 1965 to 1989, Burl Toler served as an NFL head linesman. The job requires not just the instinct to read plays as they develop and good speed, but also calmness and restraint; he was always within shouting distance of angry coaches who would let him hear it constantly.

"Burl was extremely quick; he could run like the wind," said Art McNally, former NFL supervisor of officials, when contacted by the *New York Times* after Toler's death. "But more than that he was a master of getting people who were up on the ceiling screaming and bringing them back down again."

From 1989 to 1997, Toler worked as an observer of officials for the NFL. Mike Carey, the first African American referee to work a Super Bowl (2008), who spoke at Toler's memorial service in 2009, said this about Burl: "It had to do with how to survive in the league and to flourish—doing the right things, being the right person, not being afraid of big calls, and being able to exemplify everything that comes with being an official. Burl was extraordinarily helpful to new officials."

"The name Burl Toler belongs with the true legends of not just officiating, but the entire sport," said Dean Blandino, former head of officiating for the NFL, in Schulz's piece. "He paved the way for so many officials of diverse backgrounds to realize their dream of officiating in the NFL."

Jim Tunney and Burl Toler had a unique relationship. It began in 1965 when Burl joined the NFL, was solidified when they worked together on the same crew from 1971 to 1982, and continued as good friends until Burl's death in 2009.

Born and raised in Alhambra, California, Tunney was a multisport high school athlete. Although he had the opportunity to go to a larger, more high-profile college to play basketball, he made a decision that made total sense. In a 2020 phone interview, Tunney was happy to share his memories of refereeing and his close relationship with Toler.

"I decided to go to a small college—Occidental College in Eagle Rock—because I didn't want to sit on the bench at USC or UCLA," he joked. "Plus, it was close to home." At Occidental he decided to pursue what had always been in his heart—education. "I always knew from a young age that I wanted to coach, and teach," he said. After graduating in 1951, Jim worked as a teacher, coach, and principal in Los Angeles for twenty-five years.

From 1951 to 1991, he officiated high school and college football and basketball, working in the Pacific Coast Conference. In 1960, pro football came calling. The newly formed AFL was looking for refs, and Jim's name came up. He had made an impression, apparently. "The AFL wanted me to be an official in 1960, their first year, but I held out for the NFL."

"I could handle it because I was young," he said, "and it was a privilege to be an NFL referee for thirty-one years." Ten championship games, eight divisional games, six Pro Bowls, and four Super Bowls later, as well as some of the most iconic games in NFL history—the Ice Bowl (1967), the "Catch" (1982), and the Fog Bowl (1988)—Tunney will go down as the dean of NFL referees. When Burl Toler arrived in the NFL in 1965, Jim Tunney was there. They made each other's lives better.

"It was tough for him at first—he would get some catcalls and abuse from some of the players," said Tunney. "But Burl could always handle racial issues. He never got upset that coaches were yelling at a Black man. He never mentioned any racial problems on the field, and if it ever did occur, he just rose above it. After a while, we just knew where the other would always be; if I saw a penalty, I knew that he had probably seen it first.

"In eleven years, Burl never had a problem with a call I made. He always kept his cool," Tunney said. "He was very knowledgeable about the game, about the emotions the players go through playing the game, which is very important. He never thought of himself as a trailblazer. John Madden, being a fellow Bay Area guy, was a big fan of Toler. There was a game at Candlestick Park, and right before kickoff John came busting into the referee room just to say hello. I would always tell John, 'You coach, I'll ref.'"

Burl Toler and his wife Melvia had six children. His son Burl Jr. was a Cal linebacker who helped his team win a share of the Pac-8 title in 1975 and went on to a distinguished career as an architect and project manager. USF held a special place in Burl Sr.'s heart and continues to resonate with his family, which includes three generations of Dons, said Greg Toler, another son. "USF provided our father and us with unique opportunities to chase our passion for learning and collaborating, and taught us invaluable personal and professional tools for success."

In 2013, Burl Toler's grandson Justin Carr passed away suddenly from an undiagnosed heart condition, later identified as idiopathic cardiomyopathy, while at swimming practice after school. Just sixteen years old, Justin was an outstanding student; an accomplished swimmer who competed for his school and club teams; a visual artist who created wonderful and original paintings; a budding architect who was already designing structures; an actor who loved performing; and a gifted singer with a soulful, sweet voice.

Justin was very close to his grandfather; he was thirteen when Burl Sr. passed away. In a short video made in October 2012, filmmaker Doug Harris captured Justin as he spoke lovingly of his grandfather, who had passed away three years before.

"He's touched so many people in so many different ways. He made everyone he talked to feel like they were the only person in the world. We'd go out and he'd be stopped; cars would pull over. He knew everybody and everybody knew him," Justin said in the video. "He had such a strong presence, he commanded attention," Justin continued. "I miss having someone to look up to—he always made me feel good. It's important for people to know this about him: It's one thing to do great things, but it's another to have a positive effect on people. That's what he achieved. I want to be like that. His story deserves to be told."

When Justin's mother, Susan, was interviewed, she offered these words about her father: "My dad was an educator and police commissioner in the city; my mom was also an educator and a counselor in San Francisco. We were raised on the premise that anything and everything is possible; accepting all, treating everyone equally, the difference between right from wrong, honesty, integrity, fairness, equality . . . and no bullying," Susan said.

"And the racism he encountered never stopped. He continued to stand on the right side and do his best. He did not complain; he just kept it in. I have in-laws, nieces, and nephews who accept and honor their biracial identities," she said.

In 2017, Phelan Hall at USF was renamed in Toler's honor. The building was originally named after James Phelan, a U.S. senator and SF mayor from 1897 to 1902. He railed against Japanese and Chinese immigrants and ran his campaigns on the slogan "Keep California White." USF made a change to be more reflective of an inclusive university.

"I can proudly state that my dad was an upstanding man of character from start to finish," Susan said. "He came from humble beginnings and took advantage of the opportunities provided to him. He put family first. He stood his ground. He helped and nurtured thousands of kids in the Bay Area—that's why there is a school named after him today. He did things right while not expecting any accolades.

"One of his students in junior high, Bill Yee, came to our house to deliver flowers shortly after my dad died," remembered Susan. "He said that as a child of Chinese immigrants, he often got into altercations at school and had his lunch money taken. My dad would give him a quarter for his lunch money and never called his parents when he got in trouble. Bill told me that he became a teacher because of Burl."

Here are some of the character traits that Burl preached: self-discipline, compassion, responsibility, friendship, work, courage, perseverance, honesty, loyalty, and faith. Susan also shared two of Burl's most memorable quotes:

"If you can show me a man who has never made a mistake, I will show you a man who has never made a decision."

"Treat people the way you want to be treated."

On August 16, 2009, Burl Toler Sr. passed away in Castro Valley, California. He was eighty-one. He was preceded by Melvia, who passed away in 1991. Toler was a towering figure who walked through life with humility, grace, compassion, and love.

There was a theme that ran through the different chapters of his life: team. Burl always put family first; a family is, above all, a team. On the gridiron, where he first achieved success, it was all about the team, and he became the captain. Then he became an educator; a classroom, and a school, is a team and needs a leader—he was that leader.

"I first met Burl Toler Sr. in San Francisco at a reunion of the 1951 USF football team and got to know him very well," recalled Arif Khatib. "And in 2003 I inducted him into my African American Ethnic Sports Hall of Fame in Las Vegas along with his USF teammate, NFL Hall of Famer Ollie Matson.

"After that we stayed in touch on a regular basis. He brought pride to the Black community with that appointment, and when he was assigned to be the first Black NFL official, the community was uplifted and proud. His crew partner Jim Tunney is also in my hall of fame, and we are extremely proud to have both of them. Jim and I attended the memorial service for Burl, and I was amazed at the number of people in attendance. People spoke so highly of the incredible individual who gave so much to San Francisco and to sports in general. In a nutshell, he was a giant."

Susan Carr said this about her father: "My dad did his best, and his best was sure good enough."

8

The Journey of Happiness

Billy Mills

It was getting close to race day at the Olympic Village, and Billy Mills recalled trying to get Adidas shoes from the U.S. rep so he could have some new shoes to run the 10,000 meters. In a series of interviews with the authors for this book and also for the film *Because They Believed*, Mills shared his story. He was told they were only giving shoes to "winners." Billy then told the rep, "I'm gonna win." Discouraged, upset, and with no decent shoes to run in, he went to Puma, the European rep, who gladly provided him with a pair.

It was October 14, 1964, at the Olympic Stadium in Tokyo. The twenty-six-year-old marine was there representing the United States in the 10,000-meter run, a grueling six-mile race that would often leave runners nauseous, sick, and passed out from exhaustion. For most runners, twenty-five laps around a quarter-mile track can be torture. The 10,000 meters can be a triumphant race to win, but miserable when you lose.

The 1964 race turned out to be one of the greatest finishes in Olympic history. Mills, who broke the tape with an Olympic record (28:24.4), became the first American to win the 10,000 meters and remains the only man from America to have won this race in the Olympics. The United States has not won the 10,000-meter Olympic gold since.

The 1964 race was more about endurance, tactics, and even luck than out-and-out speed. Mills, with a heroic burst that has gone down as one of the most iconic moments in Olympic and track and field history, won by almost three meters, beating his own personal best time by forty-seven seconds. "I'm flabbergasted," said Mills in victory. He also recalled that an equally flabbergasted Japanese reporter asked, "Who are you?"

Billy Mills. The spirit of the eagle.
African American Ethnic Sports Hall of Fame

The story of the 10,000-meter race at the Tokyo Games is the story of one of the greatest upsets ever seen at the Olympics. Billy Mills, a poor kid from the Lakota Sioux reservation in South Dakota, had shocked the world. Victory changed his life. And since that triumph, he has devoted much of his life to working with Native American communities.

In the book *Wokini*, a 1990 Native American allegory by Billy Mills with Nicholas Sparks, Mills describes the spiritual awakening of a young Lakota boy named David, who tells of his journey of self-awareness and the search for happiness. "David is Billy," said Mills.

In the story the boy, despondent over the loss of his sister, receives a scroll from his father containing seven pictures that hold the key to peace of mind and understanding. His search for someone who can help him interpret the scroll leads him to the Black Hills where he encounters an older man who takes David on a journey of personal discovery, showing him how each picture symbolizes a life lesson that the boy must learn. These lessons are woven into Billy Mills's story.

Billy Mills was born on June 30, 1938, in Pine Ridge, South Dakota. He is Oglala Lakota Sioux and grew up on the Pine Ridge Indian Reservation reserved for the people of that tribe. Billy did not have an easy childhood. He had eleven brothers and sisters, and when he was nine, his eldest sister who was in her early twenties died of tuberculosis. His sisters Marjorie, seven years older, and Ramona, five years older, raised him and two younger siblings. Oldest brother Sydney became his legal guardian.

His mother, Grace, was one-quarter Sioux, and his father, Sydney Thomas Mills, was three-quarters Sioux and was a tribal member. Native Americans considered Sydney to be of mixed blood. The white world called him a Native American.

"Growing up on the reservation, we were very poor, but I didn't realize how poor we really were, because I still had my dad," Billy said about his father, whom he respected tremendously. "He said, 'A lot of times your greatest strength is to be quiet.' That was the lesson I learned from him, and I carry it to this day."

Grace died when Mills was seven. His father died five years later.

"Once he died, we were introduced to poverty. I went off to the Indian schools, and once I left the reservation, I was totally unaware of the racism that I was going to face."

The youngster ran like the wind over the prairies and hills near his Lakota Sioux reservation home, trying to outrun the loss of his parents and his sister and keep the demons that coursed through his mind at bay. Mills claimed that running helped him to find his identity and to blunt the pain of rejection.

After his parents' deaths, he was raised by his brothers and sisters until he was fourteen, when he left the reservation to attend Haskell Institute, an Indian boarding school in Lawrence, Kansas, six hundred miles southeast of the reservation.

"When we were orphaned, there were really no other schools to go to. Logic was to go to some of the Indian boarding schools," Mills said. "So I chose Haskell because my older brother Walt had gone there and was on the undefeated football team and the state championship team in basketball. I thought, 'This sounds great.'"

As a youngster, Mills admired the great Sioux war chief Crazy Horse. The example of the legendary spiritual leader of the Lakota challenged him to follow his dreams, reach for goals, and succeed in life. He was a warrior who led his life through responsibility, humility, the power of giving, and spirituality. Mills tried to live by the knowledge, the wisdom, and the integrity of Crazy Horse.

"When you are happy, you will be honoring Wakantanka [the father in the sky; the creator of the world] with His most precious gift to you."

While attending Haskell, which is now known as Haskell Indian Nations University, Billy got serious about running. There his gift became more apparent as he set records in numerous track events. At eighteen he won the 1956 Kansas Class B state cross-country championship. He took up boxing and ran as a way to stay fit, but he discovered that he was a better runner than boxer and won a track scholarship to the University of Kansas, located right there in Lawrence.

The track coach at Kansas, Bill Easton, was reluctant to recruit him because he was an Indian, but he saw something in the kid that made him change his mind—namely that Billy had broken the state cross-country record by twenty seconds. It was a culture shock when he arrived on campus.

"By and large, the people in Lawrence were very respectful. Any time I needed a job, I could work an all-night shift at the paper mill. But going into restaurants and not being served, not being able to check into a hotel, well, that was bad. And it wasn't just Kansas; it was all of America," Mills said.

At Kansas, Easton told the track team, "I believe in one thing—winning. None of that 'giving it your best' or 'the old college try,'" Easton told his athletes. "No, I believe in winning." Mills excelled at cross-country while at the university, achieving All-American status three times in a row.

"I remember making All-American," Mills recalled. "I was thrilled. There were five of us, the top five cross-country runners in the country. They lined us up for a photo, and they said, 'You, the darker-skinned guy, we want you out of the photo.' I was so naive; I looked around and thought, 'What are they saying?' So I stepped out.

"The Canadian guy said, 'That's Billy Mills. He's the only American making All-American! We're all foreign athletes going to U.S. schools. I'm not having my photo taken unless Billy has his photo taken. Billy, come stand by me.' I stood by him, and they snapped the photo.

"The next year, 'Congratulations, second time. Yeah, you, the Indian guy. Do me a favor. We want to take one photo without you, and I'll take the next photo with you. I'll never know if they took one without me," he laughed as he told this story.

"Other things in society," he said. "Not being able to join a fraternity because I'm Indian. Not able to room with two good friends of mine. One was Cliff Cushman, from North Dakota, of Norwegian ancestry, the 400-meter hurdle silver medalist at the Rome Olympics."

Mills still has a letter Cushman wrote to congratulate him on his gold medal. "He wrote, 'Billy, when you won, I cried, not because of what you have achieved, but because I know where you had to begin.'" Mills said he urged the makers of *Running Brave*, the 1983 Disney movie about his life, to use that quote.

"I was upset because they did not attribute it to Cliff," Mills said. "He was Captain Clifton Cushman, U.S. Air Force." Cushman was shot down during a bombing mission in Vietnam on September 25, 1966, his body never found. He was officially declared dead nine years later.

"Another one of my good friends was Ernie Shelby, who was a 26'2" long jumper, an African American athlete from LA. We watched Ernie break Jesse Owens's record for the long jump at the Texas relays. And before they did the official measuring, the clerk said, 'Rake over it.' So Ernie lost a world record. And we were not allowed to room together, simply because one man was black, one was white, and I'm Indian."

Ernie Shelby would go on to have a fine career as a pianist, singer, songwriter, and record producer; he worked with such notable artists as Kim Weston, Three Dog Night, and the Muscle Shoals Rhythm Section.

Mills continued, "My junior year, I was All-American again for the third time. I'll never forget. I line up and I heard, 'You, Mills, congratulations, three times. Do me a favor. We want to take one photo without you, and I'll take the next one with you.'

"I was beginning to break," Mills recalled. "Society not understanding—that was just beginning to break me. I go back to the hotel room, sixth floor, and open the window. And I am on a chair and I'm leaning out. Just let go—it will all be behind me. And I'm just rolling back and forth—my knees are on the window sill; I am on a chair. Why I didn't jump? I don't know.

"I didn't hear through my ears. I heard underneath my skin the most soothing, comforting but commanding, and gentle, 'Don't, don't.' It was like my dad's spirit. I got off the chair and started crying. I wrote down for the first time, 'Gold medal, 10,000-meter run. Believe, believe, and believe.' God has given me the ability. The rest is up to me. And that is when I started training for the Olympic Games."

After graduating in 1962 with a degree in physical education, he became an officer in the Marine Corps. It was while serving in the armed forces that he qualified for the Olympic Games. Little did people know he had spent years planning for the finals. He had a profound belief that, on the day, he would break the tape.

"The Marine Corps was one of the few places I felt like I belonged," Mills said. He transferred to Camp Pendleton in California in February 1964. There he trained with the Marine Corps track team under Coach Tommy Thompson, a Canadian Olympic gold medal hurdler. But while in the marines, Mills was diagnosed with borderline type 2 diabetes. He had to learn to manage the condition so that he had enough energy to finish races.

At the Olympic trials in LA in September, he finished second in the 10,000-meter run behind high school phenomenon Gerry Lindgren. He qualified for the team in both the 10,000-meter race and the marathon but was not expected to win either race. No American had won the 10,000-meter race in the Olympics. But Mills was not discouraged. He had always lived according to the teachings of his father, who had challenged him to live his life as a warrior and assume responsibility for himself.

Mills, a believer in visualization and imagery, did not permit a negative thought to enter his head as he worked toward the biggest race of his life. He had for some time been visualizing a young Native American boy winning the 10,000-meter event at the 1964 Olympics. He created that picture in his mind over and over again. If a thought about not winning came into his mind, he would spend hours erasing the negativity.

Several elders from Mills's tribe saw him off on his trip to Japan with a prayer, "not that I would win but that I would represent myself with humility and honor my family, tribe, and the United States," he said. "It was going to be the journey, not the destination, that would heal me and give me wings to fly." Coming into Japan, he flew over Mt. Fuji, and it reminded him of the Black Hills. "It must be the heart of everything for the Japanese, I said to myself."

On that day, Australian Ron Clarke was the front-runner and favorite; he was the new world record holder, the first of eighteen marks he set in a flurry of feats in the 1960s. As a teen, he had run a sub-four-minute mile. At nineteen he was selected to light the Olympic flame in Melbourne in 1956. By 1964, Clarke was an experienced and savvy veteran runner who would take a lead early, carve out his space, and keep a blistering pace that would make other runners run out of gas.

The race had been predicted to be a three-way battle between New Zealander Murray Halbert, the defending 5,000-meter champion; the defending 10,000-meter champion, Russian Pyotr Bolotnikov; and Clarke. It did not go according to plan.

At the starting line, thirty-eight runners from twenty-three countries lined up, but only a handful thought they had a shot at a medal. Mills remembered how his father had told him, "One day you will fly like an eagle." When he lined up, there was only one thing on his mind, and that was to win.

The gun cracked and the field broke away from the starting grid. As expected, Clarke fell into first place. Halfway through the race the frontrunners separated themselves from the pack. Several runners were pushing and shoving, which allowed the leaders to pull away. Billy Mills dropped back. It appeared he was out of contention, and few paid any attention to the Native American who was well back in the field. If they had looked, they would have seen him running without effort, in perfect control, in the zone.

Mills was confident he could keep up with anyone in the world for six miles and that the race would come down to the final two laps, he said. The American was feeling the symptoms of low blood sugar, despite having eaten a candy bar before the start.

The rain-soaked Tokyo track was a wet mess, and the runners were getting lapped and were jostling each other constantly. Staying with Clarke were a gutsy Tunisian, Mohammed Gammoudi, and Mills, who at that time was a complete outsider. Although he had been a three-time All-American, on the international stage he was just an unknown who had finished second at the U.S. Olympic trials. Mills was so unheralded that, in the buildup to the Games, not one reporter had asked him a single question.

"I decided to lead a lap so I would know at least I'd led the Olympics, even if I couldn't finish," Mills said. In fact, he led more than once. The last two laps were confusion. The three leaders surged and weaved in and out of the inside lanes, passing lapped runners as if they were standing still. Clarke was looking for space while Mills and Gammoudi were trying to block him.

Entering the back straightaway for the last time, Clarke had the inside, Mills at his shoulder. Suddenly from behind, the Tunisian, Gammoudi, put one hand on each of them and with a shove sent Mills reeling and scampered between. It was such an egregious and blatant move that it could have been ruled a disqualification if he had won. Mills stepped up his pace, now closing on the two leaders.

With less than one hundred yards left, Gammoudi was now the front-runner and was running with confidence. But Ron Clarke was fading. The crowd fell silent. With the three runners speeding down the last homestretch, Billy Mills made a spectacular, totally unexpected move.

All of a sudden, like a rocket, Mills broke into a sprint, knees and arms pumping, and passed both runners, who were startled by the precocious American who had turned on the jets at the last minute. He won by three yards, setting an Olympic record.

Mills has vivid memories of his epic race. When his energy was flagging, the bird of prey reminded him of his late father's advice that "it takes a dream to heal broken wings" and gave him the willpower for a final surge to victory. He said he got through it by remembering his father's advice.

"As I went by a lapped runner, in the center of his jersey I saw an eagle, which goes back to my dad and the wings of an eagle. So I thought, I can do it . . . wings of an eagle! Thirty meters to go. Clarke and Gammoudi, then Gammoudi and Clarke, and then me. I am still five yards behind them, but I am moving fast. It was the wings of an eagle. I can win. I could see the finish line.

"During the last thirty yards as I caught both of them, my stride was better, and I knew I had another two or three seconds left in me. It was so overpowering because I thought, 'I may never be this close again. I've got to do it now . . . wings of an eagle.'

"Those words went through my mind so fast it's as if I heard them a thousand times in thirty yards. I then felt my chest break the tape, and it was so overpowering because I thought of my dad. After the race, I went to find the runner with the eagle on his jersey, but there was no eagle. There was simply a perception."

Pat Mills, his wife, was cheering fourteen rows up near the finish line, but she said she only saw her husband's hands raised in victory because the crowd of seventy-five thousand leaped to their feet, blocking the view. Officials quickly brought her down to congratulate the new champion. She said, "It was so emotional for me." Billy Mills recalled, "I healed my broken soul, and in the process, I won a gold medal."

The crowd went wild with cheering, for they had seen the impossible happen. They had just watched an underdog, a total unknown, a runner who wasn't given a chance to win, beat the favorite. They had witnessed one of the greatest upsets in Olympic history.

"My Indian roots kept me striving to take first and not settle for less in the last yards of the Olympic race. I thought of how our great chiefs kept on fighting when all the odds were against them as they were against me. I couldn't let my people down," Mills said.

After his great victory at Tokyo, Mills was honored by his South Dakota Lakota Nation with the warrior name of Makata Taka Hela. It means "love your country" and "respects the earth."

Although he was never sent to Vietnam because of his rigorous training schedule with the marines, Mills was deeply affected by the many combat deaths of men from his unit. He felt that he could not continue to participate in a sport when people were being killed in Vietnam.

Mills finished his Marine Corps tour of duty as a captain, then reentered civilian life as an official in the Department of the Interior. He followed this with a successful career as an insurance salesman. He retired from the insurance business in 1994 and became a motivational speaker, and he has been active with that and many other social causes ever since.

Mills's status as a Lakota warrior requires that he do humanitarian work. He devotes much of his time to speaking to Native American youth and to raising money for charities, such as Christian Relief Services.

"I started taking the virtues and values of our culture seriously. Find your passion and develop the skill, and this will give you direction and clarity of mind. One value I use today is truth and honesty," he said.

Running Strong for American Indian Youth is a nonprofit organization that was cofounded by Mills and Gene Krizek, founder of Christian Relief Services Charities. Running Strong operates under the umbrella of Christian Charities with the mission "to help American Indian people meet their immediate survival needs—food, water, and shelter—while implementing and supporting programs designed to create opportunities for self-sufficiency and self-esteem."

In 1976, Mills was inducted into the United States National Track and Field Hall of Fame, and in 1984 he was elected to the U.S. Olympic Hall of Fame and helped carry the Olympic flag into the LA Coliseum at the 1984 Games. In 2006, he was inducted into the African American Ethnic Sports Hall of Fame. In 2014, Mills was awarded the NCAA's highest honor, the Theodore Roosevelt Award, and in 2015 the President's Council on Fitness, Sports, and Nutrition honored Mills with the President's Council Lifetime Achievement Award.

Mills is committed to the causes of social justice and world peace. He is a voracious reader and a student of history. When speaking with him, he recounted in vivid detail, complete with names, facts, and dates, the struggle of indigenous peoples in North America, African Americans who were brought to our shores on slave ships, oppressed workers, and the struggle of women in our society for equality.

"With major obstacles in life that should not have been there, multitudes of issues will have to be resolved," Mills said, "and we have to resolve these ourselves. We are all related. What I took from sport was a true sense of unity thru the dignity of global diversity—if we choose it."

9

Running Down the Base Paths of Life

Mamie "Peanut" Johnson

Thanks to Hollywood and Tom Hanks, we learned about *A League of Their Own*, the All-American Girls Professional Baseball League, founded in the 1940s by Philip Wrigley, owner of the Chicago Cubs from 1932 to 1977. They were a collection of talented young white women who had played softball but were now playing hardball. From 1943 to 1954, fifteen teams barnstormed across the Midwest playing in front of good crowds. The perennial powerhouse was the Rockford Peaches, who won four titles.

But while that was happening, a young girl who was born in South Carolina and moved to New Jersey when she was nine was busy honing her skills on the diamond. When she was seventeen, the All-American League held tryouts in Virginia, but despite her obvious talents on the field as a pitcher and hitter, she never got the chance to play; she was African American, and the league was segregated.

This is the story of Mamie "Peanut" Johnson, who won a Negro League championship with the Indianapolis Clowns in 1954, who could trash-talk with the best of them, and who learned how to throw a curveball from Satchel Paige. A woman of indomitable will, Mamie led an exemplary life after baseball as a nurse, a youth baseball coach, and a memorabilia shop owner in Washington, DC. There is an exhibit at the Baseball Hall of Fame honoring her and Clowns teammate Toni Stone; perhaps one day their names will be in the plaque gallery at Cooperstown.

In 1941 in tiny Ridgeway, South Carolina, population four hundred, there was little else to do after school, so the boys would assemble to play baseball. But there was

Mamie Johnson. She played with the big boys.
African American Ethnic Sports Hall of Fame

one six-year-old girl who watched carefully, took mental notes, and went home and made her own baseballs out of rocks, twine, and masking tape.

In a June 2001 interview with Kevin Kernan of the *New York Post* titled "Li'l Lady Dazzled Negro League Hit Men," Johnson remembered how she first fell in love with the game. "I threw anything that had to be thrown; I was knocking birds off the fence with rocks," she said. "We didn't have basketball, we didn't have football, and we didn't have tennis. All we knew was baseball."

Her uncle Leo saw that his niece had an uncanny affinity for the game, so he taught her the proper method of catching, fielding, throwing, and hitting. "He was my friend, my everything," she said to the *Post*. Little did her uncle know that someday his determined niece would go on to play professional baseball. That little girl was Mamie "Peanut" Johnson.

When she was nine, her family moved to Long Branch, New Jersey, where Mamie played two years for the Police Athletic League. She played alongside boys, preferring the faster, rougher game of baseball to softball, typically played by girls. At twelve, Mamie joined a sandlot league and was the only girl and only African American on her team. At Long Branch High School, she played boys' sports, including football. She later relocated to Washington, DC, and, after settling in, played on all-male church and semipro teams. As she moved up, she developed into a fine all-around player, but pitching was clearly her forte. She had terrific control and could make the ball move.

She was seventeen in 1952 when she and another young woman went to a tryout in Alexandria, Virginia, for the All-American Girls Professional Baseball League, which was portrayed in the 1992 film *A League of Their Own*. Although Major League Baseball had been integrated for five years, the women's league was all white. "The coaches and players stared at us like we were crazy. They wouldn't even let us try out," Johnson recalled in the *Post* interview.

But opportunity arrived in 1953 after a scout saw Mamie, seventeen, all of 5'2", take the mound and dominate a lineup of older men while playing for a church-sponsored team in Washington. She was soon invited to try out for the Indianapolis Clowns, the famed Negro League team that launched the career of Hall of Famer Hank Aaron.

In a half season for the Clowns, Aaron, who was a shortstop back then, led the league with a .467 average and was signed by the Milwaukee Braves Class C team in Eau Claire, Wisconsin. In 1953 Aaron, only nineteen, dominated at Class A Jacksonville and started the 1954 season in Milwaukee, playing twenty-three years for the Braves there and then in Atlanta, carving out one of the greatest careers in baseball.

As African American players began to fill big league rosters, teams in the Negro Leagues struggled with attendance and quality of play. In an effort to replace Aaron, the Clowns had taken the bold step of hiring the first woman on a professional baseball team, signing Toni Stone to play second base with the team in 1953. The following year, the Clowns sold her contract to the Kansas City Monarchs. They then hired two women replacements: second baseman Connie Morgan and nineteen-year-old Mamie Johnson.

In 1953, Bish Tyson, a former player with the Negro Leagues, had seen Mamie practicing on a field in Washington, DC. He was overwhelmed by her athletic abilities and maintained that she was a great player and suggested that she play professional baseball. He introduced her to Bunny Downs, manager of the Clowns. After one tryout, Johnson made the team.

To many it seemed like a PR stunt, but not to her teammates, most of whom respected her abilities. "We had some gentlemen and some dummies who thought we didn't qualify. I worked just as hard as the fellas," she said to Eugene Meyer of the *Washington Post* in a 1999 interview. "I pitched nine innings just like everybody else. Some fellas acted ugly, but when they found out I was a ballplayer instead of some gimmick, they accepted me."

"Mamie could pitch, and Toni could hit," onetime teammate Gordon Hopkins told Meyer. "It was no joke. It was no show. Somebody hit the ball down to Toni, Toni threw you out. Mamie, she was good. We had to respect the girls, be on our p's and q's, and the girls respected us." And the man who caught most of her games agreed. "I was proud to catch 'Peanut' from 1953 to 1955," said Art "Junior" Hamilton.

The Clowns won a championship in 1954. From late 1953 through the end of the 1955 season, in her three-year stint with the Clowns, Mamie would go on to rack up an impressive record of 33-8 on the mound while averaging a more than respectable .276 average at the plate. The Clowns were the last of the Negro League teams to disband, continuing to play exhibition games into the 1980s.

She earned the nickname "Peanut" while pitching her very first game with the Clowns, against the Birmingham Black Barons. In Kernan's 2001 piece, we learn how she acquired that distinctive moniker. A trash-talker, Hank Baylis, hollered from the dugout that she didn't "weigh no more than a peanut, so how could she strike someone out?" When he stepped to the plate, Mamie's wicked curveball whiffed him, and the nickname stuck. She was known as "Peanut" from then on. A deceptively hard-throwing right-hander, she threw a fastball, slider, circle change, screwball, and curveball, for which she received pointers from the great Satchel Paige.

Her earlier rejection by the women's league, she said, was a blessing in disguise. "If I would have played with the women," she said in a 2003 radio interview with NPR, "I would have missed out on the opportunity that I received, and I would have just been another player. Now I am somebody who has done something that no other woman has done." Her baseball career was cut short when she had a son.

After her baseball career, Ms. Johnson, who had attended New York University to study engineering and medicine before signing with the Clowns, studied nursing at North Carolina A&T State University and worked as a nurse at Sibley Memorial Hospital in Washington, DC, for thirty years; she also coached youth baseball and conducted baseball clinics.

When she retired from nursing, baseball continued to play a major part in her life. She spent the rest of her life educating adults and children about her time as a ball-player in the Negro Leagues. She was the manager of a Negro Leagues memorabilia shop in Prince Georges County, Maryland.

Indianapolis mayor Stephen Goldsmith declared April 3, 1998, Mamie "Peanut" Johnson Day in Indiana's capital. "Whereas she serves as a role model to what hard work and determination can achieve," the proclamation reads, "the City of India-napolis takes this opportunity to salute a true American athlete." In 1999, Johnson was a guest of Bill Clinton at the White House.

In 2008, Johnson and other living players from the Negro League era were symbolically drafted by major league franchises prior to the 2008 MLB draft, and

Johnson was selected by the 2019 world champion Washington Nationals. In 2009, she spoke at Baseball Americana 2009, organized by the Library of Congress. A baseball field at the Rosedale Recreation Center in northeast Washington, DC, was named in Ms. Johnson's honor in 2013. And in 2015, a Little League named for Johnson was formed in Washington.

"To me it was nice," she told the *Washington Post* of her baseball barnstorming years, "because I saw things and places I never would've seen. It was a tremendous thing to wake up and look out the bus window and be 500 miles from where you were before. It was gorgeous. I enjoyed it. They were the three best years of my life. The pay was very skimpy. I think I made, like $300 a month, plus $2 a day for food. If you were going to make a living playing baseball, you'd starve to death. Oh no, we played for the joy of the game, and I enjoyed all of it, believe me."

In 2014, Mamie met Mo'Ne Davis, a then twelve-year-old Philadelphia girl who pitched her team into the Little League World Series that year, and the first Little League baseball player to appear on the cover of *Sports Illustrated*.

"Well at the time I just thought it was cool that she was a pitcher," said Mo'Ne in a piece on MLB.com titled "The Negro Leagues' Only Female Pitcher," "and then basically she was one of the only female players, and that I was a girl and that I was a pitcher. I thought that was the coolest thing ever."

Johnson was a fixture in Davis's life after that first meeting, and she even attended the ceremony when Davis's Little League jersey was inducted into the Baseball Hall of Fame. Davis, who played second base in softball at Hampton University, says she's thankful for that support and hopes to carry on Johnson's legacy.

"She was just always there," Davis said. "No matter where I turned, she was kind of there at something big that I was having. So, I always say thank you. It's one thing that I'll probably keep thinking about and later on in life try to do the same thing for girls that are coming up."

In the *Washington Post*'s obituary for Mamie in December 2017, it said that Johnson talked about Davis. "She reminds me of me," Ms. Johnson said at the time. "I wasn't no baby doll. No girlie girl. Baseball was all I knew. And I loved it." Mamie "Peanut" Johnson died at the age of eighty-two in 2017, leaving behind several siblings, her husband, Emanuel Livingston, six stepchildren, nineteen grandchildren, and five great-grandchildren. There is currently a petition circulating, created by Andrew Farley in conjunction with MoveOn.org, to induct Mamie into the National Baseball Hall of Fame. It reads as follows:

"Mamie 'Peanut' Johnson, Toni Stone, and Connie Morgan were the only three women in American baseball history to ever play in a men's league. Yet, they are not in the Hall of Fame. Mamie Johnson was the only female pitcher to ever play with the men. These women deserve their spot in history as well as their spot in the Hall of Fame. The entire All-American Professional Girls League (a league of all white women) and thirty-five Negro League players (men) have been inducted into the Hall. It's time Mamie was given her rightful honors."

Arif Khatib has many fond memories of Mamie.

"When I inducted Mamie into the African American Ethnic Sports Hall of Fame in Las Vegas in 2003, along with Dr. José Sulaimán, president of the World Boxing Council (WBC); Don King; Althea Gibson; Burl Toler; and Ollie Matson, Mamie said, 'This ceremony gives me the opportunity to meet some of the world's greatest sports legends. I feel like royalty.'

"Mamie spent time visiting with everyone, especially Evander Holyfield, who seemed to enjoy talking with her because he didn't know there were female baseball players in the Negro Leagues. Race car driver Willy T. Ribbs was also there, and folks were thrilled to meet him. There was no shortage of filmmakers present; one crew was shooting a film about Don King, another from PBS was filming a special on Mamie's life, and Don King Productions filmed the ceremony for broadcast on his network.

"After Mamie returned to Maryland, we talked at least once a week, and she would refer to me as her 'boyfriend' and would ask to speak to her boyfriend when she called. She was one of the funniest people I've ever known. She said she'd spent some time in Oakland with Toni Stone and felt that Oakland was her second home and wanted to come back and visit. I invited her, and she came for several days.

"She told me about her special friendship with Satchel Paige and that he was sweet on her. He told her he would teach her how to throw a curveball, and they had fun while barnstorming on a bus where she was the only female. Mamie said she would tell jokes with the players. And of course she told me about how she got her nickname.

"I visited her whenever I was in the DC area at her memorabilia shop, and we would visit some of her family and friends. I asked if I could have a young female baseball phenom I knew at the time call her because I thought the meeting would be good for both of them, and she agreed to do that. To listen to her talk about the 'good old days' of baseball was so enjoyable; here I was with the only female pitcher ever in the Negro Leagues, learning about her unique experiences.

"As her health began to deteriorate, I had more difficulty reaching her directly, so I would call her daughter, and Mamie would call me back. I monitored her health closely and would speak to her husband occasionally until her death. I was saddened to hear of her passing but will always have a place in my heart for a baseball trailblazer who was not only a great player and competitor, but a better person."

10

The Joy of Flying

Archie Williams

The 1936 Berlin Olympics are best remembered by Americans for two things: African American track athlete Jesse Owens winning four gold medals and Adolf Hitler refusing to shake Owens's hand. The significance and symbolism of Owens winning those medals cannot be overstated; he was the man who shattered Hitler's myth of Aryan superiority. But he was not the only gold medal–winning African American athlete at the Games. One of Owens's teammates recalled:

"It was like a railroad track, and I could see where it would be very easy to step out of your lane. Then I got into the straightaway, I had a little lead but I managed to hold them off. It was kind of a blur, because it was so much noise and excitement and yelling and screaming. So I just tried to block that out of my mind and just concentrate on running a good-paced race." That excerpt is from a 1992 oral history conducted by Gabrielle Morris for the University of California Black Alumni Series titled "The Joy of Flying: Olympic Gold, Air Force Colonel, and Teacher."

That teammate was a twenty-one-year-old University of California track star named Archie Williams, who won the gold medal in the 400-meter run.

"I was happy," Archie Williams recalled in another oral history he did in 1988 with the Amateur Athletic Foundation of Los Angeles (AAFLA). "Initially, you're kind of numb. You have to pinch yourself to say, did I really do that? Then it kind of sinks in. Somebody once asked me, 'How does it feel to be the greatest in the world?' I said, 'What the hell are you talking about? How do you know I'm the greatest in the world?' I said, 'I just beat the ones that showed up that day.' So I have no illusions about this 'greatest in the world,' because there's nobody that's the greatest. Maybe for one moment he might be."

Archie Williams. Going for the gold, Berlin 1936.
Courtesy of Marin History Museum

"It was like a dream," he offered in the 1992 Cal oral history. "What am I doing here? Is this me? One year I was nothing, the next year I was in this. Here you are in front of the whole world and they're playing 'The Star Spangled Banner.' You see your name up on the board. Then they hand you the medal. The next day I said, 'Gee whiz. Was that really me?' It was a great feeling."

Nine years later, after Europe was rent asunder, countries destroyed and tens of millions killed, America finally shattered Hitler's dream of a Nazi empire. But there are still burning embers from that conflagration, and we must be vigilant if we are to avoid another resurgence of those authoritarian impulses as they gain traction in the twenty-first century. And it helps to learn the stories of the individuals who were present when this history took place, for they not only witnessed it; they made that history.

Becoming an Olympic champion was only the beginning for Archie Williams. He went on to earn his degree from Cal in mechanical engineering and became a pilot.

During World War II, he was a flight instructor for the famous Tuskegee Airmen, the first African American combat pilots in history, and earned the equivalent of a master's degree in meteorology to become a weather officer.

After the war, Williams had a distinguished career as an air force officer, including service in combat in Korea. He then went into education as a beloved high school mathematics and computer science teacher for more than twenty years. And in 2021, that school, in San Anselmo, California, honored him by renaming Sir Francis Drake High School, built in 1951, Archie Williams High School.

African American athletes realize that sports are a vehicle that breaks down barriers and fosters greater understanding and goodwill. Some of our most effective goodwill ambassadors have come from our athletic ranks. These athletes were committed to helping America become a better nation. One was Archie Williams.

Archie Franklin Williams was born in Oakland, California, on May 1, 1915, the son of Wadsworth and Lillian Williams; he grew up in Oakland and Berkeley, the oldest of three children, with a brother and a sister.

His grandfather was in the army, stationed in the Presidio in San Francisco. When he got out of the army, they moved to Oakland. In the 1920s and 1930s, Oakland was a far different place than it is now. In 1930 it was less than 4 percent African American. Many of the families who arrived in the 1930s were transplants from the Dust Bowl states. Between 1940 and 1970, Blacks fled the Jim Crow South to seek better opportunities in California.

Tens of thousands of these migrants came to Oakland, drawn by the promise of plentiful jobs in a city at the center of the region's expanding wartime economy, bolstered by an infusion of federal defense money for shipbuilding and the construction of the Oakland army base and naval supply center and the shipyards in nearby Richmond. The largest influx of African Americans into Oakland came during this Second Great Migration, and by 1980 the city was 47 percent African American. The city is now a vibrant, diverse city that has blossomed in the past few decades.

The Oakland that Archie Williams grew up in was a family-friendly place. Archie's father was from Chicago. He had a grocery store in Oakland, and he bought real estate. It was a safe place for a kid to grow up, and a place for a kid to dream.

"I was born on May 1, 1915," Archie remembered in the AAFLA oral history. "We had a typical three-kid family, nothing unusual to talk [about]. We moved about five times over a period of ten or twelve years. So I had a chance to live in north Oakland, west Oakland, east Oakland, Berkeley, south Berkeley, and north Berkeley. So I felt that I had a larger number of friends than I would have had otherwise. At that time, the Depression hadn't quite started yet—I think my dad had a car. It certainly didn't seem like we were rich, but yet we never suffered for anything."

Archie's father died from pneumonia when Archie was only ten, and he grew up in a house with strong women, the dominant force being his grandmother, who was an early civil rights activist; she was involved with the NAACP during the 1920s when the Ku Klux Klan was at its peak. The NAACP periodical *Crisis* was the first magazine Archie ever read.

One of the Berkeley parks Archie and his friends went to would not let them swim because their skin was the wrong color. There was a sign that said "no Black people." That must have been a shock for people coming from the South, for they had been told that things were better out in California.

"Well, we can laugh about it now," he continued in the AAFLA oral history, "but at that time, practically anything that had any sort of social implication was affected by the racial situation. For example, restaurants where you couldn't be fed, theaters which you couldn't attend, no public swimming pools, and organizations like the Boy Scouts and the YMCA. In fact, we had a so-called colored YMCA, which was nothing more than an old house with a couple of pool tables. All my friends, who were mostly Caucasian, wanted me to be in the Scouts, but I was told I wasn't eligible—for obvious reasons."

Archie attended University High in Oakland. He had grown up playing sports informally and discovered that he had a knack for sprinting, winning makeshift 50-yard dashes regularly. Word got out that he was really fast. He was also the top quarter-miler around for his age group; when he went out for the track team in high school, his reputation preceded him.

When he graduated in 1933, it was the middle of the Depression, and there were no jobs to be had, especially for an unskilled young Black man. A friend suggested they enroll at San Mateo Junior College because it was free. So they traveled across the bay, went to an area near the school, and found a lady there who had a little place in the backyard. They could stay there for five dollars a week, including breakfast.

Williams recalled in the Cal oral history that he asked his friend what he wanted to be, and the friend said, "A dentist." "'Well, I'm going to be an engineer.' We both laughed about it. Well, it turns out eventually both of us made it." So he enrolled and started taking courses.

He joined the track team and found a role model and mentor in the San Mateo track coach, Oliver "Tex" Byrd. Byrd was supportive and encouraging to Williams. Archie was running the 50-, 100-, and 220-yard dashes, but he was not getting the times he wanted. So Coach Byrd encouraged him to try the quarter mile, because he thought Williams's stride was right for it. And he also encouraged Archie to aim to transfer to a four-year school.

"In 1934, there weren't any Black athletes at Stanford. Byrd made a real effort to get me accepted there, but to no avail," Archie recalled in the 1992 interview with Morris. "Coach Byrd told me, 'If you were white, I could get you in just like that.

And get you a scholarship.' The only Black guys at Stanford were washing dishes in the frat houses," Archie said. "And I never got beat by one of those Stanford guys."

Byrd followed his athletes' grades, in part because he sent nearly all of them to four-year programs, notably Stanford and USC. Williams, though, went to Cal in spring 1935 as a sophomore bent on academics. In those days, he observed, schools often recruited, then redshirted Black athletes, merely wanting to foreclose on their playing for opposing teams.

Later, when reflecting on this period, Williams did not mince words about his feelings for USC. The Trojans had been accused of recruiting African American athletes during the 1930s just to keep them away from Cal and UCLA, but then refusing to let them play. Williams described in the 1992 interview with Morris how he always wanted to go to UC Berkeley:

"I could stand on the front porch of my grandfather's house, look right up Telegraph and see the Campanile (tower). . . . I saw that and I wanted to go to that school. I think it was destined that I go to Cal. We used to go up and sneak into where the track guys were practicing and crawl under the fence and watch the real athletes perform. I was kind of born a Cal man."

Williams did not go to Cal to play sports; he went for an education and a degree, preferably in a major that would lead to an engineering field. Archie wanted to be a mechanical engineer. When he was younger, he had won a prize in the *Oakland Tribune* model airplane contest. He didn't need an athletic scholarship to attend Cal. Tuition was only $26 a semester, and he could live at home with his family.

"That was my goal because nobody in my family up to that time had ever gone to college," Williams said in the AAFLA interview. "Not that they felt that I was obligated to do it, but it was something that I felt was a good challenge and worth trying. At least I could say that I did it."

So he enrolled at Cal for the fall semester in 1935 as a sophomore transfer. Cal's respected track coach, Brutus Hamilton, had never heard of Archie until he showed up for tryouts. But Williams made the team, and in Hamilton he found a coach and teacher to whom he would remain close until Hamilton's death in 1970.

Williams's first priority was always academics, and Coach Hamilton supported all the track athletes in that. Hamilton got extra respect from his athletes because of his own experience, having won a silver medal in the decathlon at the 1920 Olympics in Antwerp.

Williams was unknown when he started running for Cal. But under Hamilton's tutelage, his talents blossomed. His junior year, 1936, would be his breakout year. Before then, he had never run the 400 meters in less than forty-nine seconds. But during that year he ran faster and faster until, at the NCAA championships in Milwaukee, he not only won the 400 meters but set a new world record with a time of 46.1 seconds.

But racism would rear its ugly head again. He spoke with his college counselor who told him that he should be realistic about job prospects after graduation. The two fields the counselor mentioned were being a preacher or a real estate agent, because a Black man couldn't get hired as an engineer.

In the spring of 1936, Cal faced off against the competition at the Long Beach Relay: USC, Stanford, and other colleges. He beat all of them in the 400 meters, so when the NCAA games took place in Chicago, he was ready—and he won. Williams's victory there gave him an automatic berth in the Olympic qualifying meet in New York City two weeks later.

It was a huge adventure for Archie, who had never been east of Reno. He was accompanied by Coach Hamilton, who was an assistant coach for the Olympic team. Brutus Hamilton was more than a track coach; he was also a fine baseball player who had a tryout with the New York Yankees, an amateur boxer who many said could have fought professionally, and an accomplished English teacher. His style was ahead of his time. He would not nitpick your form; rather, he'd encourage his athletes to just do their best and never disparage their opponents.

Williams finished first in the 400 meters at the 1936 Olympic trials with a blistering time of 46.8, just under his world record, and two weeks later he was on a ship headed to Berlin.

Despite the Nazi racial policies that were already in effect in Germany in 1936, Archie and the other African American Olympic athletes were treated very well by ordinary Germans, better than they were used to in the United States. But he was well aware of Adolf Hitler's feelings about Blacks and Jews.

The 400 meters was one of the last events of the Games. For two weeks before his race, Williams practiced in the mornings and then watched the track events in the afternoon to root for his American teammates. He especially admired Jesse Owens from Ohio State, who was known as the "Buckeye Bullet."

One year before, on May 25, 1935, Owens achieved track immortality during the Big Ten meet in Ann Arbor, Michigan, setting three world records and tying a fourth. At Ohio State, Owens, who had been born in Alabama, had to live off campus with other African American athletes. And when the team traveled, Owens had to eat at "Blacks only" restaurants and stay at "Blacks only" hotels.

On the ship, they put all the Black athletes together in the same stateroom, and then all together in the Olympic Village. To Archie it didn't matter at first; these guys were all his friends. But to Archie it was like the folks in charge were saying, "We want to make sure that you are with your own kind."

"Then we got on the train and to Berlin, and they took us out to this beautiful area—it looked like a country club—where the Olympic Village was," Archie recalled in the AAFLA history. "They had it landscaped, and all the buildings were brand new. It was set up with cottage-type barracks. Every country had its own dining hall, and since we had one of the largest teams, we had all the goodies."

In Berlin, Owens won his fourth gold medal in the 400-meter relay when, at the last minute, head coach Lawson Robertson replaced Jewish American sprinters Marty Glickman and Sam Stoller with two outstanding college sprinters, Frank Wykoff and Foy Draper, to run with Owens and Ralph Metcalfe. Owens had initially protested the last-minute switch, but as Alan Abrahamson of the *LA Times* wrote in 2001, assistant coach Dean Cromwell said to him, "You'll do as you are told." The American relay team then went out and obliterated the world record.

Glickman blamed Olympic director Avery Brundage and Cromwell for the switch, claiming that they sat the two Jewish runners for two reasons: Cromwell's public anti-Semitism and his favoring Wykoff and Draper because they ran for him at USC. Glickman knew that Brundage was also an anti-Semite and did it to please Hitler.

When it was his time to race the 400-meter run, Archie Williams was ready. The starts are staggered in the 400 meters, with two turns, making it difficult for runners to know exactly where they stand in relation to the other runners for much of the race.

It was a very close race. Williams won the gold with a new Olympic record of 46.5 seconds, although that was four-tenths of a second slower than his own world record. The silver medalist, Englishman Godfrey Brown, finished just two-tenths of a second behind him. And Archie's American teammate James LuValle took bronze, one-tenth of a second behind Brown.

When asked who handed him the medal, Williams's sense of humor came to the surface: "Some French guy," he said in the Cal oral history. "They wanted to kiss you. Get out of here! They'd hand you the medal and a scroll. It was sort of like graduating."

Hitler refused to shake the hands of Owens, Williams, and other Black medalists, although he did congratulate some of the winners, even saluting them one day. The Olympic Committee then informed him that if he was going to shake hands with some of the winners, he would have to shake hands with all of them. Hitler did not like to be told what to do—especially in his own backyard.

When asked in later years, Williams laughed: "Hitler wouldn't shake my hand either!"

And when asked how the Nazis treated him, he replied, "I didn't see any dirty Nazis, just a lot of nice German people. And I didn't have to ride in the back of the bus over there."

Realizing that shaking hands would mean being seen as publicly acknowledging Black and Jewish athletes, Hitler childishly refused to congratulate anyone, although he met with all the German winners privately in his box. He was especially upset by the success of the African American runners, eight of whom won medals.

Hitler said at the time that the Americans should be ashamed of themselves, letting Negroes win their medals for them. Tragically, many Olympians would lose their lives in the war, including six Jewish Olympic medalists who would be killed in the Holocaust.

After the Olympics, the athletes went back to England for an exhibition race. From London they went to Amsterdam, Rotterdam, Norway, and Sweden. Jesse Owens had returned home already, so Williams ran the 100 meters during the exhibitions. At an exhibition in Stockholm, he ran the 100 without warming up and injured his hamstring. It did not heal properly, and when he returned to Cal the following year, he reinjured it several times.

When he returned to the Bay Area, Archie was greeted with a parade and was given the key to the city and a gold watch from Oakland. After a welcome back to campus that included a noon rally, Williams continued with his engineering studies and became the first African American to run for the university's student council. Williams was also a member of the Alpha Phi Alpha fraternity. But, although he continued to have success on the track, he was never able to return to his 1936 level of performance.

Archie hit the books hard after this, making up for the time he had lost in preparing for the Olympics. He had the résumé: Olympic champion with a degree in mechanical engineering from UC Berkeley. But because he was African American, he could not get a job. Echoing his childhood love of planes, he became interested in aviation and tried to sign up for a civil pilot training program at Cal, which was sponsored by the government. At first the program turned him down because of his race, but Coach Hamilton interceded. Archie was admitted.

Unable to find employment as an engineer, he began working at Oakland airport, fueling planes and washing windshields. He went through the training required to be a flight instructor, but no flight school would hire a Black man for that job, so he made a living giving private lessons to student pilots and eventually got his pilot's license.

In 1940, Williams heard that the Army Air Corps had begun a pilot training program for Black soldiers, so he applied to be a civilian instructor. At that time, there were not many Black pilots in the country, and only a handful who were licensed as instructors. So his application was accepted immediately, and he became an instructor with the first class of Tuskegee Airmen, the first Black pilots in the history of the American military.

Tuskegee had a civilian program. They had training facilities and pilots. First Lady Eleanor Roosevelt went down there to observe. Impressed, she pushed hard to set up a training program for military pilots. When the United States entered World War II in 1941, Williams joined the reserves while continuing to train pilots at Tuskegee.

Williams spoke with pride about his experience with the Tuskegee pilots. "The greatest thing in my life was to prove Blacks could fly airplanes and become officers," Williams told Cal. "Skeptics said that 'the jump from the plow to the plane is too much for these coons.' We were supposed to fail; they expected us to fail. The gold medal means a lot to me, but there are more important things in my life."

When he was called to active duty in 1942, he asked to become a pilot. Despite the fact that he was already a trained pilot, the army told Williams that he was too old (twenty-seven) for pilot training. Upon discovering that he had an engineering degree, the army sent Archie to a one-year course at UCLA in meteorology. The course was the equivalent of a master's degree. At the end of the course, Williams was commissioned as a second lieutenant in the U.S. Army Air Forces. He returned to Tuskegee to perform his work as a weather officer. While there, he was finally allowed to become a rated pilot and began teaching instrument flying to the cadets.

After the war, Williams decided to make a career in the military. When the U.S. Air Force was established as a separate branch of the military in 1947, Williams became one of the original officers. His decision to make a career in the military was bolstered when, that same year, President Harry Truman issued an executive order desegregating the military.

"Truman was our main man," Williams said in the CSM centennial newsletter. "He was the one who integrated the military. They found out that [segregation] doesn't make sense. Since I had training in both flight and weather, I would jump in that plane and check the weather. I used to go up and fly around and see how the weather was, call back, and say, 'It's okay to fly.'"

And with that order, Williams became eligible for the first time for a position that would place him in command of white airmen, opening many new opportunities for him. After four years as an officer, Lieutenant Williams was finally entitled to walk into an officers' club.

In 1948, Archie, now thirty-three, was admitted to the prestigious Air Force Institute of Technology, and in 1950 he attained a degree in aeronautical engineering. During the Korean War, he was stationed in Japan as a meteorological officer. Although the air force considered him too valuable to be risked in combat, he talked his way into flying combat bomber missions over Korea.

Williams served twenty-two years in the air force, retiring in 1964 as a lieutenant colonel. During his last year, he decided that he wanted to teach after he retired. While stationed at Strategic Air Command in Riverside, he applied for the teacher credential program at UC Riverside.

Remarkably, he was denied admission because he did not have a specific math class that was a prerequisite, despite his engineering degrees and meteorological training. Williams called his old friend Brutus Hamilton, who was still the head track coach at Cal. Once again, Hamilton interceded, and Williams was admitted to the program. He got his teaching credential the following year.

After his retirement from the air force, Williams returned to the Bay Area, where he got a job teaching mathematics at Sir Francis Drake High School in San Anselmo, in Marin County north of San Francisco. At fifty, he became a high school teacher and also coached the track team. He taught at Drake for twenty-two years.

"I taught at Sir Francis Drake High School, which is an average-sized high school, nothing different from any other school," Williams said in the AAFLA article, describing his last career. "The kids were real nice, and they had a lot of school spirit. It's in San Anselmo, which is sort of in the middle of Marin County. It's a good cross-section of the county. There was some affluence and some poverty, and a good ethnic mix. It was a nice place to work because it was just small enough to where you knew everybody. And you got to know the people in the community real well, so you felt like you were part of something."

Later, as computers began to become essential, he taught computer science. He was a beloved teacher, especially focused on working with kids who were handicapped or slow learners.

In 2021, the former principal at Drake, Liz Seabury, when petitioning the county school board to rename the school, spoke glowingly of Archie.

"Thank you for recognizing Archie," Seabury said. "It is an honor to name our school after such an important person for our students to emulate. Archie Williams's contributions and character align beautifully with the student body's values. My hope is that the board will see this recommendation as a true and just move toward a name that recognized community, equity, positivity, and service to others. That's what Archie Williams's remarkable legacy says to us."

Archie's son Carlos passed away in 2022. He had spoken at the 2021 ceremony that named the school after his father: "People have told me for years that my dad was a living history lesson. Teaching was his greatest passion. He would be so pleased to be honored in this way."

"We are so glad he was able to see the high school named in honor of his father," added Tara Taupier, Tamalpais Union High School District superintendent.

One former student, Rose Malliett, said, "I was blessed to have him as my teacher for four years." Another, Rose Milani, said, "He was a great teacher. I am honored to have had the opportunity to know him."

And from Christopher Weills, editor-publisher of *The Ultimate Sports Guide*, "As a graduate of Archie Williams High School in San Anselmo, I remember Mr. Williams being discussed appreciatively and held in high regard. I am thrilled the school now bears the name of this important African American."

Williams finally retired in 1987 at the age of seventy-two. He and his wife, Vesta, whom he had married when they met at Tuskegee during World War II, continued to operate a flying service that they had run part time for several years.

In 1986, he was one of the original inductees into the Cal Athletic Hall of Fame, and in 1992 he was inducted into the USA Track and Field Hall of Fame. In 2003, Archie was inducted into the African American Ethnic Sports Hall of Fame.

Archie Williams passed away on June 24, 1993, in Fairfax, California, at the age of seventy-eight. He is survived by his son Archie Jr., a well-known jazz and blues guitarist. His was an amazingly full and impressive life.

Carlos's wife, Sheila, shared her memory of Mr. Williams. "Carlos worked as a school crossing guard for a while, and absolutely loved it because it gave him the opportunity to be with children, and his dad would have been very happy about that," she said.

Carlos told her, "He didn't talk much about his military career, but mostly about education. He lived to teach, and that was his most important undertaking. Everyone spoke highly of my dad, who had strong feelings about people with learning disabilities. They were very comfortable in his presence because of his patience with them."

Archie is not well known by most people, unless they happen to be followers of track and field. His athletic achievements and his leadership demonstrated how an African American could fight his way through the challenges of racism to become a national hero. In addition to his many athletic accomplishments, he was a contributor to society in general.

Archie's commitment and sense of purpose was driven by a strong desire to be the best he could be among the many endeavors he set out to conquer. And clearly he succeeded. And, like many other athletes of color, he pushed the envelope. He arguably was the best of the best.

Archie and his contemporaries were subjected to inhuman and cruel conditions that could have left the impression they were not talented enough to be among America's greatest athletes. But they were determined to succeed against all odds. They ran through the obstacles placed in their paths to glory. And now their achievements are irrevocably enshrined in the pantheon of American sports.

11

Sistas on the Links of Love

Janet Johnson

In 2007, Janet Johnson had a revelation and then an idea, one that was borne of tragedy but has become one of nurturing, love, and hope. In an interview with the authors, she spoke at length about her organization, Sistas on the Links, and the motivation behind it.

"After my only son passed away in 2007 from lupus, I was devastated, walking around in a fog, and one of my colleagues noticed I was unfocused," Johnson said. "A fellow golfer and coworker who had also lost a child told me at the time that the only thing that was able to give him back his focus was golf. I decided to join a club, looking for a place to play and to heal, and play with other women. When I went out on the course, I immediately felt the sun, the fresh air, the joy. I was playing at Blue Rock Springs Club in Vallejo [California], and I saw a flyer in the ladies' room looking for women golfers. After playing two rounds with some members, they said I could join the club.

"Well, normally when you play a round, you're with the same three golfers for three or four hours, so naturally you converse, and you often talk about family. But it never came up during these rounds," Johnson said. "I felt isolated. The other golfers were virtually always white women, and there was not much in common. I realized that I wasn't having fun.

"And when I wanted to have some of my friends join this club, I was told that they were capping the membership at seventy-five members—and I was the seventy-fifth! I didn't feel wanted, and I felt like a token. I knew that what I needed was to be nurtured and healed by being in the company of Black women. And other Black women who played this game needed the sisterhood.

Janet Johnson. Golfer, innovator, and sister.
Courtesy of Janet Johnson

"Initially I was going to start a pickup group to play every week, but I realized that I as well needed the sisterhood. If I started a club with Black women, we could support each other. The idea for an all-women's golf club came to me immediately," Johnson recollected. "We all felt the isolation, not belonging, like how did we get here? There was strength in numbers, and constant nurturing. I could walk on the course with other Black women and feel empowered."

In 2008, Janet Johnson went into action. She founded the nonprofit organization Sistas on the Links Women's Golf Club (SOTL), whose five-point mission is clearly stated:

1. Unite and expose African American women to golf.
2. Provide opportunities to play in an environment of encouragement and acceptance.

3. Strengthen our golf skills.
4. Support each other in reaching our personal goals through networking, mentoring, and social activities.
5. Introduce golf to young women and nurture their academic growth.

In a short period of time, Johnson has seen membership swell to over eighty, governed by a board of directors that consists of seven officers and appointed chairs of standing committees. In 2009, SOTL became a member club of the Western States Golf Association (WSGA). In a conversation with Janet, she expounded on their five-part mission:

1. Unite and expose African American women to golf:

"I thought it was important to make the game more open and more available to women, especially African American women. Historically, these are two groups who have had hardly any access to the golf course. With our organization, we are changing that. One of our goals is to introduce women to the game of golf and support their learning experience."

2. Provide opportunities to play in an environment of encouragement and acceptance:

"I needed the nurturing, and I got it. And so have many other women. Our club is only available to African American women. Men cannot be members—just women. I am so happy that I helped to establish the club. It helped me heal, gave me a soft place to land and to be nurtured. It is an environment of safety. The joy and confidence I feel is great. We have so many women who see and understand this. In SOTL, we are all about helping women feel comfortable on the golf course, including playing the game and learning the language, rules, and etiquette."

3. Strengthen our golf skills:

In SOTL there are many women who have never picked up a club. They encourage people to participate, and if you're a beginner, all the better. Janet expounded on some of the ways the club does this.

"We encourage people to take lessons. There are several resources available to folks who want to learn, at local courses, community colleges, and clinics. And practice, practice, practice. Golf takes commitment. You'll see the improvement in your game.

"Don't be afraid to come out and play with the club," she added. "We provide a safe place to play and learn. Be prepared to keep the game moving, even if it means you have to pick up your ball. And watch and learn from experienced members. Don't be afraid to ask questions. Learn and always use proper golf etiquette when out on the course."

4. Support each other in reaching our personal goals through networking, mentoring, and social activities.

Recently retired as the economic development administrator for the city of Richmond, Johnson's background is in business, banking, and lending, and she has definitely put those skills to use developing and supervising the growth and expansion of Sistas on the Links.

"Everyone knows that deals are made on the golf course," she said. "No one ever made these women feel comfortable on the course. Women did not know how to approach the game. With our help, now they do. I had just retired, and I never saw Black women on the golf course. I thought African American women should be exposed to the game. Their husbands or significant others did not make them feel interested or welcome in the game. This was a place where we could unite these women and expose them to the game."

5. Introduce golf to young women and nurture their academic growth by supporting youth golf development programs—and give back.

SOTL is involved with First Tee of Northern California, whose goal is "to impact the lives of young people by providing educational programs that build character and instill life-enhancing values through the game of golf."

For twenty-three years, First Tee has been using golf to provide learning opportunities for young people. Their programs are offered at courses, elementary schools, and youth centers in all fifty states and delivered by coaches who have been trained in positive youth development.

"Our members are actively involved with First Tee," Janet continued. "We volunteer at local venues and work with young girls at several courses in the East Bay. This is a population that we want to support. Golf is not cheap. These children can't afford clubs, shoes, greens fees, or tournament fees, so we reimburse the families for those expenses.

"A portion of the dues we pay goes to raise money for these girls," Johnson said. "We want to teach them and get them into high school sports. SOTL gives them opportunities for college. "We've had girls go to caddy schools and get paid for summer jobs caddying for NBA (Golden State Warrior) players.

"This year we had several high school seniors receive golf scholarships at colleges. One will be attending Prairie View in Texas; another is going to Long Beach State, one to the University of Nevada at Reno, and one to UC Davis. These girls spoke at a Zoom meeting recently. It was heartwarming—and it makes me want to cry to think about them and what they've accomplished."

Today, HBCUs (historically Black colleges and universities) are in danger of losing their golf teams. About half of the women players at these schools are white—because the schools are looking to be competitive and there are not enough African American students who have had the opportunity to excel on the links. Janet Johnson wants to change that.

Lynda Donahue is a retired educator, having worked for thirty-eight years, including twelve years as the special education director in the Vacaville Unified School District. She was an original member of SOTL, is currently an officer of the club, and also serves as tournaments director. In 2016, Lynda was elected to the board of directors of the Women's Golf Association of Northern California (WGANC).

"As a charter member of Sistas on the Links, I am thankful for the dedication and foresight of Janet Johnson," said Lynda in a phone interview recently. "Janet brings enthusiasm and a sense of joy to the game of golf. Being in SOTL is like being in a sorority of golfers. This club has provided an opportunity for women of color to experience an activity that was once closed to them. It is a goal of SOTL to provide access to golf and golfing experiences in a safe environment.

"I like the mission of SOTL, which is to mentor and support young girls. The Little Sistas program is also a part of the Northern California Golf Association Youth on Course program. Youth on Course offers access to golf for five dollars a round at courses nationwide," Lynda continued, "and for the second year in a row, I will participate in the Youth on Course fund-raiser called '100 Hole Hike.' I will play one hundred holes of golf, and I am asking donors to give to the Youth on Course efforts to provide scholarships and internships to young aspiring golfers."

Among other things, Sistas on the Links is focused on providing access to organized, convenient golf in a friendly learning environment, and offering organized golf events and player development opportunities for both beginning and experienced golfers.

"Country clubs have historically not been open to African Americans. We tell women that we take people at all levels. We have two kinds of memberships," Janet Johnson explained. "An associate membership, which is only fifty dollars a year, is for people new to the club. There is no handicap with your score; you are learning—often from scratch—and we encourage you to take lessons and do clinics that we hold once a month. We pair the 'newbies' with the experienced members. We walk and talk with them on the course and teach as we go—we're here to help you."

For the more experienced golfers, there is a full membership ($100 per year), which also includes membership in the WSGA, the sixty-seven-year-old and most established African American golf association operating primarily in the western United States.

In addition, full membership also includes the Golf Handicap Information Network (GHIN), a service offered by the USGA to golf associations worldwide. GHIN is one of the largest handicap management tools in the world, serving more than nine million golfers. It helps members seeking to play in sanctioned tournaments. Sistas on the Links sponsors the following programs:

- Nine-hole play days—monthly, open to all members
- Eighteen-hole play days—monthly, open to all members
- Dine and Wine—monthly nine-hole play, lunch, and networking
- Clinics—monthly, focused on mechanics, rules, and golf
- SOTL annual tournament
- WSGA member club tournament announcements
- Sista Golfer of the Year
- Little Sistas program—tournament, travel, educational support

Sistas on the Links has participated in many tournaments and found success. "We've had four tournaments where we had to turn people away," said Johnson. "In addition to our local club, we joined the WSGA. There are thirty-three WSGA clubs in six states," she explained, "and there is an annual tournament. We [SOTL] became the first all-women's club to win the overall championship in 2017, and we won in 2018—the first to win back-to-back titles.

"Some of our older members are going back to school—and golf took them there. We have a sixty-something-year-old woman enroll at Napa College, and out of that experience she learned how to compete and win, and she got a scholarship at Jackson State to play golf," Johnson said with pride.

Sistas on the Links is based in Richmond, California, in Contra Costa County, rich in Black pioneer leadership and culture, including the nation's oldest and arguably most well-known park ranger, the recently retired centenarian Betty Reid Soskin. Bisa French is the Richmond chief of police, and Richmond native Pumpsie Green was the first African American to play baseball for the Boston Red Sox.

Diana Becton, a former trial judge, was sworn in September 2017 and became the first African American to be elected district attorney in the history of Contra Costa County. She is also a member of SOTL. In a conversation with DA Becton, she described how much the organization means to her.

"I am so glad that I connected to the Sistas on the Links women's golf club," Becton said. "This extraordinary group of women offers a truly friendly, supportive, and welcoming place to learn and play the game. All levels of players are truly embraced, those who have never held a club as well as those who are experienced golfers. In addition to finding a warm and amazing sisterhood, I have learned about the rules and the etiquette of golf. I am especially proud of our support for youth. My Sistas assist in teaching young golfers, and we offer financial support for the development and education of our youth. I love my SOTL!"

DA Becton also weighed in on the criminal justice system. Here's what she said:

"It's a new day, and I represent a change from the status quo. We cannot keep doing the same things repeatedly with regard to prosecuting cases or incarcerating individuals. We need to support policies to end mass incarceration. Being a progressive district attorney means I care about the safety of my community just as much as a traditional prosecutor or law enforcement official. To effectively administer justice, we must demand that everyone be treated fairly and independently. We must never stop working to eradicate racism and bring about systematic change throughout all systems, especially in our criminal justice system. I will continue to fight for criminal justice reform not only in Contra Costa County but throughout this nation."

Looking back on all that she has accomplished, Janet Johnson feels a tremendous sense of pride and satisfaction, but her mission is hardly complete. When asked about her decision to establish SOTL, she said this:

"I am happy about it because it has helped me with my healing, helped me to form a group of women who looked like me, who related to what I was going through, gave me a safe place to grieve, a safe place to heal, and a safe place to play golf. It's a relaxing experience, an environment of faith.

"The night before a tournament, it feels like Christmas. I wake up joyful; I can't wait to get out to the course. I am in awe when I see these women get out of their cars, get their bags, and put their shoes on. No one feels like they don't belong."

With Sistas on the Links—and love—Janet Johnson has found herself and her sisters.

12

The Man Who Risked It All

Curt Flood

Of all the unsung athletes we talk about in this book, perhaps none had a greater impact on other athletes than the late Curtis Charles Flood, who passed away in 1997. His courageous and eventually triumphant stance in 1969 against the reserve clause of Major League Baseball opened the door for free agency in not only baseball, but the other major sports as well. He risked everything to stand up for his right to choose for which team he would work in his chosen profession.

Curt Flood was not just facing down the history of baseball's uniquely oppressive no-trade policy, which was inextricably interwoven with its equally onerous antitrust exemption; he was facing down endemic racism, which had prohibited hundreds of otherwise qualified Black athletes from playing in the major leagues for fifty years until Jackie Robinson entered the major leagues in 1947.

Marvin Miller, then executive director of the Players Association, told Curt he didn't have a chance of winning the celebrated case, which went all the way to the U.S. Supreme Court, and that Curt would most likely be blackballed. In a 2011 piece for the *Atlantic* titled "How Curt Flood Changed Baseball and Killed His Career in the Process," sportswriter Allen Barra described Flood asking Miller if bringing the case would benefit other players. "I told him yes," said Miller. "'And it will help those who will come after you.' Curt said, 'That's good enough for me.'"

Because of the pressure exerted by that suit, Miller was able to bargain for the right to grievances. And in 1975, when white pitchers Andy Messersmith and Dave McNally agreed to play a season without a contract, after that season they were ruled free agents. By that time, Curt Flood had walked away from baseball and was running a bar in Majorca, Spain. But he was a winner—and so were those who came after him.

Curt Flood. An artist on and off the field.
African American Ethnic Sports Hall of Fame

Curt Flood was an outstanding baseball player, a center fielder who played fifteen seasons in the big leagues for the Cincinnati Reds, the St. Louis Cardinals, and the Washington Senators. Flood was a three-time All-Star, a Gold Glove winner for seven consecutive seasons, and batted better than .300 over a full season six times. He tied for the National League lead in hits (211) in 1964 and in singles in 1963, 1964, and 1968. He also led the National League in putouts for a center fielder four times and in fielding percentage as a center fielder three times. He retired with the third most games in center field (1,683) in NL history, trailing only Willie Mays and Richie Ashburn.

Flood became one of the pivotal figures in baseball's labor history when he refused to accept a trade following the 1969 season, ultimately appealing his case to the U.S. Supreme Court. Although his challenge was unsuccessful, it brought about solidarity among players as they fought against baseball's reserve clause and sought free agency. This led to the restructuring of the reserve clause and officially ushered in the current era of free agency, which has proved incredibly lucrative to players in all sports.

But it's what Curt Flood didn't do in 1969 that helped change the game forever; he did not accept a trade.

Cardinal management, despite the fact that the team had won the National League pennant and had taken the Detroit Tigers to a game seven in the 1968 World Series, offered Flood a meager $5,000 raise for the 1969 season, this coming on the heels of a season where Curt hit .301 and won a seventh consecutive Gold Glove.

After the 1969 season, and after over a year of bad blood between Flood, his teammates, and Cardinals ownership, general manager Bing Devine wrote a letter to Flood informing him that he had been the key piece in a multiplayer trade with the Phillies. On October 7, 1969, St. Louis traded Flood, Tim McCarver, Byron Browne, and Joe Hoerner to the Philadelphia Phillies for Dick Allen, Cookie Rojas, and Jerry Johnson. Flood refused to report to the Phillies, citing the team's poor record and dilapidated Connie Mack Stadium and what he believed were belligerent—and racist—fans.

Flood said he was not going to report to Philadelphia, mainly because he did not want to move to another city. Some reports say he was also irritated that he had learned of the trade from a reporter; but Flood wrote in his autobiography that he was told of the trade by mid-level Cardinals management and was angry that the call did not come from general manager Devine, further alienating him from owner Gussie Busch, multimillionaire heir to the Anheuser Busch beer fortune.

Thus, despite his long and outstanding playing career, Flood's greatest legacy was achieved off the field. He believed that Major League Baseball's decades-old reserve clause was unfair in that it kept players beholden for life to the team with which they originally signed, even when they had satisfied the terms and conditions of those contracts. He was the first to advocate for free agency.

So that fall Curt met with Phillies general manager John Quinn, who left the meeting believing that he had persuaded Flood to report to the team. Flood stood to forfeit a $100,000 (equivalent to $800,000 in 2023) contract if he did not report, but after a meeting with players' union head Marvin Miller, who informed him that the union was prepared to fund a lawsuit, he decided to pursue his legal options. Below is Flood's now famous December 1969 letter to Bowie Kuhn, preserved in the National Archives.

"After twelve years in the major leagues, I do not feel I am a piece of property to be bought and sold irrespective of my wishes. I believe that any system that produces that result violates my basic rights as a citizen and is inconsistent with the laws of the United States and of several states. It is my desire to play baseball in 1970, and I am capable of playing. I have received a contract offer from the Philadelphia club, but I believe I have the right to consider offers from other clubs before making any decision. I, therefore, request that you make known to all Major League clubs my feelings in this matter, and advise them of my availability for the 1970 season."

In December 1970, after sitting out the entire 1970 season, Curt Flood refused a trade to the Washington Senators, but he eventually signed a contract with them. In April 1971, Flood played only thirteen games for the Senators and then retired from the game. In December 1975, baseball's reserve clause was struck down by arbitrator Peter Seitz in a case involving white pitchers Andy Messersmith and Dave McNally. The following July, owners and union agreed to a labor contract that included free agency. Flood, despite being the driving force behind the victory, spent the remaining twenty-one years of his life getting little recognition from baseball or the hall of fame.

In September 1998, the Curt Flood Act was passed by the Senate, establishing antitrust law protection for baseball players to the same extent as other professional athletes. In February 2020, led by Congressman David Trone of Maryland, 102 members of Congress signed a letter to the Baseball Hall of Fame advocating for Curt Flood's induction.

PERSONAL REMEMBRANCES OF A FRIEND

"There were many people who influenced my life," said Arif Khatib, "but none more than Curt Flood. It became a defining moment in my life when I met him in the 1980s. I was at a reception for Orlando Cepeda, and there was something about Flood that got my attention. After Curt spoke, I approached him and told him that although I was never a baseball player, I was a true baseball fan and knew of his history and sacrifice.

"I told him I followed his career and was very much aware of his refusal to be traded from St. Louis to Philadelphia. I had an opportunity to talk to him for a few minutes at the reception and asked him where he lived, and he said in Oakland, off Fifty-Fifth Avenue. Curt was born in Houston but moved to Oakland as a boy. He had played in the same outfield at McClymonds High School as Vada Pinson and Hall of Famer Frank Robinson. Curt later transferred to Oakland Tech.

"He said to call him sometime. I said I would love to do that and discuss his case because I was a history buff and was thinking of writing a book and doing a film about sports, and he would definitely be part of that idea. He gave me his phone number and I called him. He said, why don't you pick me up and let's go for a drink and talk. He chose a date, gave me his address, and I picked him up—amazed at how many times I had passed right by his duplex on Fifty-Fifth Avenue. I had a cousin who lived about fifteen blocks away. I passed his duplex every time I visited her, which was quite often.

"So that day we went to a club on Grand Avenue and talked for more than two hours. He said he liked talking to me and that it gave him a big lift and asked if we could do it again. Of course, I said. Sometime after that I called him and said let's get together again. This particular time, he said, 'Just stop by the house. We can talk here.' That started a friendship that lasted several years until his untimely death in 1997. I was not a high-profile athlete, or someone I thought he would want to engage in conversation about his career in baseball, but he said that I seemed to have a firm grasp of the subject that most people didn't.

"He shared with me some of his paintings he did while living in Spain. I am not sure many people knew that Curt was an accomplished professional artist/painter and sold many pieces of his work to museums and individuals. Since he no longer was a pro ballplayer with a six-figure salary, his paintings were how he made money, and he did well. After learning more about his tremendous loss of income from not playing baseball and being blackballed from the game he loved, I told him I thought it was truly an admirable sacrifice by a person who wanted to make a difference in society and help other professional athletes.

"I was introduced to his wife, actress Judy Pace, while attending an event in Los Angeles he had invited me to. That gave me an opportunity to meet his son and two daughters, who were instrumental later in helping me induct him into my African American Ethnic Sports Hall of Fame. Curt was inducted posthumously in 2006 at a ceremony at the Hyatt Regency in San Jose, along with several other athletes: Julius Menendez, John Henry Johnson, Willie McGee, Lincoln Kennedy, Don Johnson, Yoshihiro Uchida, Irene Obera, and Gene C. Johnson. There I was able to see for myself how much this man was loved, and not just by his family, but by people of all ethnicities, from all walks of life. Judy accepted on his behalf.

"While Curt was still alive, I promised him I would do all I could to let the world know about his sacrifice for other athletes. I have spoken to many athletes since, and I have been surprised by how many do not know who Curt Flood was. Bill Patterson, former director of Oakland Parks and Recreation, told me of a plan to name a park after Curt, and I immediately jumped in to support that effort and spent considerable time working on the project.

"I met a number of times with the director and attended the official naming of a park and baseball field now known as Curt Flood Field in the Dimond District of Oakland, three minutes from where I live today. After that, I wanted to keep my promise to Curt and began to tell as many people as I could about this amazing man and the field named after him.

"As a way to help bring local, national, and international attention to the park, I suggested to the City of Oakland that they consider an annual event to be named the Curt Flood Platinum Award Ceremony. Since a platinum award carries more weight than a gold award, a select committee would choose the top athlete for each year from baseball, football, basketball, hockey, tennis, track and field, and other major sports to receive and be presented the award as part of a weekend of activities, including a sandlot baseball game at Curt Flood Field. Funds generated by the ceremony would be earmarked for the improvement and maintenance of the field."

To date, Curt has not been inducted into the Major League Baseball Hall of Fame—and that is shameful. Moreover, for the multitudes of pro athletes—not just baseball players—who benefited financially beyond their wildest dreams from Curt's sacrifice, the sporting world owes it to his memory and his legacy to step up. What better place to honor his contribution than Oakland, his hometown?

His family is circulating a petition encouraging the hall of fame to induct one of the most courageous and brilliant athletes ever.

Curtis Charles Flood died on January 20, 1997, two days after his fifty-ninth birthday. Jesse Jackson delivered the eulogy, which stands as his epitaph: "Baseball didn't change Curt Flood. Curt Flood changed baseball. He fought the good fight."

13

Breaking through to Awesome

Dr. Tae Yun Kim

KOREA 1950

"Bombs were exploding all around me. My family had just left me behind, all alone in this chaos. I was five years old. Yet, because I was a girl, an extra mouth to feed, I was considered bad luck. I was left all by myself, left to die. I was screaming for my mother; I was so scared. They stuck me in a corner and told me to stay behind. I couldn't understand why they all left.

"An old man came running by and felt sorry for me and had me run with him. But it was hard to keep going with my short legs, and I had to stop. Then a girl who was a few years older than me came running by and said, 'If you stay here, you will die. Come on, I'll race with you!' In the midst of this inferno, someone, for the first time ever, was nice to me. It was the sweetest voice I had ever heard.

"All of a sudden, a bomb exploded right next to us and I lost consciousness. When I came to, I was looking for the girl. When I found her, she was lying still on the ground and bleeding all over. I shook her, screaming, 'Wake up, I promise that I will run faster. Wake up!' Then I noticed that her arms were gone. She never woke up.

"That was when I made a promise to myself. I told myself I will not run any longer. I will not hide. I knew in my heart that I had a purpose to fulfill and nothing was going to stop me. I was better than that."—Dr. Tae Yun Kim, from her 2018 book, *Seven Steps to Inner Power: How to Break through to Awesome.*

Martial arts grandmaster Dr. Tae Yun Kim was born in South Korea just after World War II. Starting at the age of seven, she defied five thousand years of Korean tradition prohibiting girls from practicing martial arts and, against all odds,

Tae Yun Kim. Breaking the mold.
Courtesy of Tae Yun Kim, Lighthouse Worldwide Solutions

overcame physical, mental, and social obstacles to achieve what everyone claimed was impossible.

She moved to America as a young woman and founded the *jung suwon* style of martial arts. She is the first female to attain the rank of great grandmaster in taekwondo. Through hard work and despite unimaginable obstacles and challenges, she became the first female grandmaster in the history of Korean martial arts. She is also a successful entrepreneur and CEO, author, lecturer, motivational speaker, and teacher.

She incorporates her dedication to excellence, high energy, and can-do spirit into a philosophy that has served her and countless others well. Who is Dr. Tae Yun Kim? She is one of a kind, a true original. She's been called Wonder Woman, a phoenix rising from the ashes, a force of nature, and a living legend. She breaks traditions and fulfills her dreams. This is her remarkable story.

Grandmaster Kim's life is the quintessential rags-to-riches immigrant success story. Tae Yun Kim was born on February 2, 1946, on the Lunar New Year. Everyone was expecting her to be a boy. Her family considered it catastrophic that their firstborn child was a daughter, and she was the curse of the village. Her alcoholic father beat her daily. She was neglected, starved, and blamed for all of her family's hardships. This would be the first of many obstacles Grandmaster Kim would face in her life.

"I was abandoned from the moment I was born; my mother pushed me to the corner to let me die," said Kim in her 2018 book. "My grandmother said, 'Oh my God, our family has been cursed. We're doomed. Let this girl die; turn her over to suffocate her!' Lucky for me, my mother couldn't bring herself to kill me."

After the war, she reunited with her family. Nevertheless, from the time she was a child, Grandmaster Kim broke with tradition. Like all Korean girls, she was expected to learn to cook and sew, have her family find her a husband, have twelve sons, and then maybe her bad luck would be gone. They never gave any chance for a different life to girls. Five thousand years of culture and tradition dictated these things, and nobody before her questioned them. But she was different from everyone else, even at a young age. She already knew that the power was in her and that it was her personal choice what she did in her life.

One morning, when she was seven, she witnessed her uncles practicing taekwondo in the morning mist. She knew at that moment, "This is what I want to do. This is my future." And right away she begged them to teach it to her.

They laughed at her, "Hey, you are a girl!" They said, "Girls can't do that! It is forbidden to girls to train in the martial arts. Go back into the kitchen and learn something useful." One of her uncles, the youngest one, agreed to teach her. His plan was to keep hitting her so hard during practice that she would quit. To his surprise, she stuck with it and improved.

Her grandparents were very upset and immediately wanted to marry her off, so they invited the village matchmaker to their home. But instead of daintily serving tea, something the matchmakers watched carefully to see how skilled or how clumsy a girl was, she purposely dumped hot tea on the matchmaker, which sent the message that she was a tomboy and not ready to ever get married.

Her grandfather was furious. As a last resort, he asked the local Buddhist monk, a very revered man, to take her to a monastery and lock this crazy girl up for life. Instead, the monk started to train her in the true ancient martial art, which is the art of unifying body, mind, and spirit. She trained hard and progressed quickly, with a laser-like focus. In her book, Kim explained how she was able to do that.

"My childhood circumstances—being resented by my mother, beaten by my father, shunned by my entire village, and laughed at for aspiring to be a martial artist—would have overwhelmed me with self-pity had my teacher not taught me to take charge of my own life and refuse to be a victim. He taught me that my own thoughts create my own reality, what I think and what I can accomplish."

After the death of one of her brothers, Tae Yun and her family sought a fresh start in Burlington, Vermont, in 1969. Now twenty-three, with just $300 to the family's name, she was determined to open her own martial arts school but faced immediate challenges.

In the 2021 documentary film *Because They Believed*, produced by Arif Khatib, Kim recounts that period in her life:

"So, even though I didn't know any English, I go to America, full of excitement, this was meant to be a new start, new opportunities in the land of hope and glory," Kim recalled. "But reality was very different. One of the first things I did was to go to the local high school to convince the principal to hire me to teach martial arts. But nobody would talk to me, and nobody would give me the time of day. I had my dictionary, my notepad, my pencil, and I'd sit in the hallway. Every day I go and I know that door would be open someday.

"All of the boys and girls looked at me like I was from another planet. At that time on the East Coast, there were hardly any Asian faces. They called me all kinds of names, like you smell, you stinky. They would yell at me to go back home to where I came from. And whenever I didn't understand what they were saying, I'd just smile and say, 'You too.'"

When she finally got to talk to the principal about her idea to be a martial arts teacher, he put up roadblocks, saying he was worried that kids would get hurt. Bruce Lee was big then, and they were put off by the violence in his films.

"No, I am going to teach these students how to break through their mental barriers," said Kim in the film. "I am going to teach them confidence and discipline, and how to stay focused and be positive." When they heard that, they relented and gave her a chance. Within months, her class was the most popular at the school, and she was voted teacher of the year. The fearless little (4'11") girl from war-torn Korea was starting to succeed in her new life.

But she still maintained her incredible work ethic. She got a job at Howard Johnson's and worked at a gas station on weekends.

"I was cleaning toilets in hotels, but I was so excited. I worked, and I got paid. Back in Korea, I would work all day and all night and would only get beaten. Now I was making money! People ask me all the time, when did you get so successful, and my answer always is, 'When I was cleaning toilets.' Why? Because I knew that this was only a stepping stone for bigger and better things.

"I'd walk around the neighborhood, write my name, and I'd say, 'Hi, my name is Kim. I want to be your friend.' Sometimes I knocked on a door, and there'd be a shotgun, a really mean face. I walked to one hundred houses—only three were open. That was the prejudice I had to deal with."

Nobody would rent her a space for her martial arts school. After struggling to teach and still doing other odd jobs to pay the rent, she was finally able to open up her own school. She was so excited and worked hard to pay the rent. But her dream literally went up in flames when a jealous, racist person set fire to her school, and again she lost everything. America was definitely not like the vision she had in her mind, but she persevered.

After several years of struggling to make her vision a reality, she didn't want to keep living like that. She took her Bible and climbed up a nearby mountain to fast and pray and hoped that God would grant her wish to let her die.

But God did not let her die. While on the mountain, she had a vision of technology and of helping people through that technology. Kim thought she was just hallucinating after fasting because she knew nothing about computers. She came down from the mountain and continued with her life. Two months later, she had the vision again, and this time she wasn't fasting. This was not a hallucination. This was a direct sign from God.

But she still didn't know anything about business, and even less about technology. So she invited her top student to start up this company with her. In her book, she recalled that at first he laughed at her, saying that she did not know a thing about computers, and why would she want to start such a business? But she didn't give up, and in 1982 she started Lighthouse Worldwide Solutions.

Her first project was to produce video games based on Bible stories. Why video games? When she was teaching martial arts, she noticed that most of the kids had calluses on the palms of their hands, and when she asked what caused them, they told her it was from the joystick in playing video games.

She was so excited when they created their first video games, about Moses, Samson and Delilah, and more. But they still needed to market the games. They gave away everything, including the source code of the program. Because none of the great grandmasters team knew anything about business, they never charged any money and came back empty-handed. She also realized that small, rural Vermont was not ready for her innovative ideas, so in 1985 she moved to Silicon Valley, where her company started to grow.

Eventually she developed her own branch of martial arts, calling it "jung suwon," which means the way of uniting body, mind, and spirit in total harmony. The purpose of the art of jung suwon is, in Kim's words, to "give you practical tools to free yourself from limiting, self-defeating states of mind."

Within a short period of time, she built up her martial arts school, and it became one of the largest in California. She has helped thousands of people, among them CEOs and world-class athletes, achieve success in the martial arts.

Black belt testings at Jung SuWon Martial Art Academy present unique challenges to candidates. Grandmaster Kim tests not only physical abilities but the mental and spiritual abilities of her students. They have to perform physically in the *dojang*; they also have to go through a very special outdoor program on their own. They must also perform community service and write a dissertation.

Kim is always asking them for the unexpected. For example, while waiting for a plane departure at a busy airport, she asked a black belt candidate to execute a difficult form, or pattern, right then and there, with crowds of people all around. The student would have to be able to say, without even a trace of hesitation, "Yes, ma'am," and go for it.

As her school and business continued to grow; she was featured on TV shows, gave keynote speeches, and started her own TV talk show and the TYK brand clothing company.

When Grandmaster Kim performs ki energy demonstrations, she sometimes does seemingly impossible things. There are videos of her walking on flames and lying on beds of nails and standing and moving on raw eggs without breaking one of them. Who would ever believe that this tiny woman can do all of this? How does she do it? And, more importantly, why?

She does this purely to perform *nae gong*—internal power.

"Did you know that we all have this power in us? We just don't know it," Grandmaster Kim wrote in her book. "We just have to learn how to use it, how to harness this power and apply it in our personal, daily lives."

To prove her point, when she gives lectures and wants to demonstrate this concept of inner power, she always picks the weakest, oldest, or smallest audience members. She often has them break boards—not the thin demonstration-type boards, but the full-sized pine boards.

She has them write down their goals on that board. For her, there is no such thing as just breaking a physical board. They will be breaking through some kind of mental barrier that is holding them back. By transferring her energy to the person and making them realize they have that energy, they are able to break right through.

"That power is available to all of us, and we need to use it in our daily lives," continued Kim. "This is why I have become successful, because my master taught me how to use this power and apply it. It is not just meant for martial arts; you can use it for anything in your life."

Her company, Lighthouse Worldwide Solutions, took off with the vision of creating a business that would serve businesses and people globally. Lighthouse's goal to continually produce and deliver products that make a positive impact on people's lives starts with Dr. Kim's personal philosophy of positive and proactive thinking.

The list of her accomplishments is very long. Dr. Kim has received countless awards for innovations, as well as the Susan B. Anthony Award for California Woman of the Year. She was named "Hope of the Country of Korea" by then-president Kim Dae Jung during the IMF crisis in 2001, when so many people lost their money and jobs, and worst of all, they had lost all hope.

The suicide rate in Korea spiked very high; Kim went on a monthlong lecture tour to give people hope and a new life. She was flooded with letters of gratitude, and thousands of people changed their minds and realized they didn't have to end their lives; there was so much joy still ahead. Her positive spirit energized the whole country.

In 2004, when the world was experiencing an economic downturn, she was awarded the Grand Prize of the California Chamber of Commerce in a contest titled "Simply Essential Success Stories" for running the most innovative business in California. During a time when others downsized their business, when they let go of their best workers, Great Grandmaster Kim was there to hire them and expand her business.

In 2009, Grandmaster Kim received knighthood into the Orders of Constantine the Great and of St. Helen, the first woman ever in the 1,700 years of the history of the order to receive knighthood. Their vision is to enhance society through leadership, and their mission is to recognize men and women who share their belief in chivalry and in the power of faith, hope, and charity. Their objective is to help disadvantaged, abused women and children of the world with their temporary needs, without distinction of color or creed and at no cost to them or their families.

In 2021, Grandmaster Kim broke five thousand years of tradition again when she, as the first Korean female to ever train in taekwondo, accepted appointment by the Kukkiwon World Taekwondo Headquarters to be the global ambassador for Kukkiwon. For this male-dominated organization to honor a woman with this responsibility was historic.

Great Grandmaster Kim has a mission to share the spirit of taekwondo with the world using her own life example of overcoming and rising above impossible challenges to achieve success in her life. This once-in-a-lifetime recognition by Kukkiwon is historic because women have always been second-class citizens in Korea. Dr. Kim has broken through the glass ceiling and has helped open doors for women training in the martial arts and has inspired women and all people to overcome the challenges in their own lives.

Her biography is taught as part of the curriculum in South Korean schools. She is a much sought after motivational speaker and has spoken at several universities and in many countries. Wherever she goes, whatever she does, she always shouts out her personal motto, which is invariably shouted right back at her by the audience, young or old:

"He can do. She can do. Why not me!"

In the film, she explained the simple guidelines she lives by, and how she follows her own voice.

"Don't let anyone steal your dreams. I didn't," she said. "You have the power to fulfill your dreams. Remember, you must take charge. Nobody can eat for you, drink for you, or go to the bathroom for you, or sleep for you. You have to do it yourself."

In 2018, Kim published the book *Seven Steps to Inner Power: How to Break through to Awesome*, which describes her philosophy and the spiritual force that guides her. It is much more than a "self-help" book. Rather, it is a comprehensive, well-written, well-organized guide to breaking through every obstacle to achieve our goals, a step-by-step manual for personal growth and empowerment. Inside the pages of this book are contained simple yet profound messages.

The seven steps to inner power:

1. Bring together your body and mind as one.
2. Seek the truth in ourselves and the world around us.
3. Cultivate purity.
4. Learn to love ourselves with a pure, accepting, and spiritual love.
5. Develop commitment and loyalty to ourselves and our growth.
6. Sacrifice, through which we eliminate unnecessary activities and make decisions about where to spend our time, energy, and money so as to achieve our goals.
7. Develop patience with ourselves and others.

Dr. Kim's top ten precepts to live by:

1. Self-discovery means learning to live free.
2. Your own thoughts can be your worst enemy.
3. Self-love.
4. Change.
5. "I can't" usually means "I won't."
6. Before you can express love, you must find love.
7. Let go of self-condemnation and guilt.
8. Forgive.
9. Use your will to conquer fears and weaknesses.
10. Physical training is mental warfare.

In 2010, Dr. Kim founded the TYK Foundation. With her motto of "He Can Do, She Can Do, Why Not Me!" the foundation helps individuals, families, and communities improve their quality of life by offering support to those facing hardship; helps people succeed in their lives and personal goals; and teaches people to take charge and become leaders to improve their own lives and the lives of those around them.

Recently, Grandmaster Kim was asked a few questions about the state of martial arts, her philosophy, and her own amazing journey.

How would you say martial arts have changed since you started your school?

"Martial Arts are more accepted today. When I first started my school, many people thought that the martial arts were violent. For years, they only saw them in second-rate movies, and it was very aggressive and bloody. At that time, most schools were little dinky places tucked behind malls, and people were hesitant to enroll their kids or themselves.

"Later on, movies like *The Karate Kid* started to show the true power of ki energy in a way that was easy to see, and more people wanted to start training to improve their lives. Still later, martial arts often got embedded into trendy movies, such as *The Matrix*, and training in the martial arts became a 'cool thing.'

"At my school, I have always focused on teaching the traditional philosophies of the martial arts. Taekwondo is not just about kicking and punching. It is a way of living. This is how I have always taught my students. When I started training, I was the only girl in the martial arts, as it was forbidden for women. Today, women and girls freely train, and the numbers are growing. Martial arts are mainstream, and people value and appreciate its countless benefits."

Judo has been an Olympic event for a while. Do you think taekwondo or any other martial art has a place in the Olympics?

"Of course! What better way could there be to promote taekwondo? Millions watch the Games on TV. My role in bringing taekwondo to the Olympics started back in 1978 with the First Pre-World Games in Seoul at the Kukkiwon World Taekwondo Headquarters.

"I was the head coach for the first U.S. women's taekwondo team, and we brought back gold, silver, and bronze medals. The Olympics are the world's recognized games for athletes of all backgrounds to showcase their talents and abilities. Because there are so many different styles of martial arts, each with their own unique characteristics, I believe they should all have the opportunity to compete against others in the world and to showcase each of their specialties."

Your belief in making every challenge an opportunity for positive change and growth has been the driving force behind the success of Lighthouse. Is there anything you'd like to add to this?

"Yes. However, I don't claim to have done this by myself. Without God as my guide, I would have ended up like every other girl at my time. I would have never been able to achieve anything without Almighty God. God has given me a very strong belief in making every challenge an opportunity for positive change and growth, and this has been one of the main driving forces behind the success of my life.

"I always say, 'Rejoice in the lessons of pain and hurt.' It gives you strength. It gives you freedom. My entire life from the moment of my birth has been filled with challenges. I have learned that in order to move forward in life, I could not and will not let myself become a victim of my circumstances, a victim of my environment. This is why I tell people that it doesn't matter where you come from, who your parents are, what your economic or social class status is—you have the power to change your life. The power is in you. It is your personal choice what you do in your life."

You have been a strong supporter of veterans. Tell us about that.

"I am a Korean War survivor. At the age of five, I was abandoned by my family and left to die during the war. It was the U.S. soldiers who came to save me, my village, and my country. Without them, I would not be here today. I truly owe my life to them. I remember so well how we were always starving; there was never enough food to go around. We would stand in long lines at the local army base, just for a small cup of powdered milk.

"To us, it was a matter of life and death. These soldiers not only fought for our country but also gave us food for survival. Whenever I can, I honor veterans. Several times I have had ceremonies to award Korean War veterans a special medal that was constructed from the barbed-wire fence that is at the Demilitarized Zone (DMZ) between South and North Korea.

"The men and women who serve in our armed forces sacrifice their own personal comforts to protect our country, to protect the citizens of this beautiful United States of America. They are selfless and courageous when they are on the front lines of war. I salute each one of them, and I will continue to support veterans in any way that I can."

Great Grandmaster Dr. Tae Yun Kim has spent her life *Breaking through to Awesome*. She wants to help others do the same.

"I will continue to teach and help people accomplish their dreams, through whatever means God shows me," Dr. Kim said. "Nothing brings me more joy in my life than when I can help people. All these amazing things I have accomplished through God, with God, and for God. Without God, I am nothing, not even a speck of dust."

14

Legend of the Long Jump and the Law

Edward Gourdin

He was born in Florida in the nineteenth century and entered Harvard just as the United States was entering World War I. In 1921, while competing at track for the Crimson, he set school records that after one hundred years still hold up. It was there that he became the first man in history to reach twenty-five feet in the long jump. He went on to win an Olympic silver medal in 1924 in the long jump and then came back to get his law degree from Harvard.

He enlisted in the National Guard in 1925 and became the commanding officer of the 372nd Infantry, a segregated and decorated regiment. He rejoined the National Guard after his discharge in 1947 and retired in 1959 with the rank of brigadier general, the first in Massachusetts for an African American. And in 1958, he was sworn in as the state's first African American superior court justice. Edward Gourdin was a trailblazer, an American original.

A headline from the *Boston Post* on Sunday, July 24, 1921, read, "Harvard-Yale Overwhelms English Rivals." It went on, "Ned Gourdin, Harvard's outstanding Negro athlete, broke the long standing record for the broad jump when he cleared 25'3", a mark which promises to stand for some time."

On the day before, at the Harvard/Yale versus Oxford/Cambridge meet held at Harvard, Gourdin defeated Englishman Harold Abrahams—who was later chronicled in the beautiful 1981 Academy Award–winning film *Chariots of Fire*—in two events. One was the 100-yard dash.

"Colored flier starts event by nailing first event on card," the *Post* said later in their article. "At the crack of the gun Gourdin was away like a flash, but as the tape was reached Abrahams made a herculean effort to pass the fleet crimson runner, who won by inches with a time of 10.2 seconds."

Edward Gourdin. From the cinders to the courtroom.
African American Ethnic Sports Hall of Fame

The other event Gourdin shined in that day was the long jump, which he won while setting a then world record of 25'3", shattering the existing record by almost three feet. This was the first legal long jump over twenty-five feet. "It was considered almost impossible," trumpeted the July 24, 1921, issue of the *New York Telegram* of his jump. As we will learn here, nothing was impossible for Edward Gourdin.

Edward Gourdin was born in Jacksonville, Florida, in 1897, one of nine children. His father, Walter Holmes Gourdin, a meat cutter, was part African American and part Seminole Indian, and his mother, Felicia, was African American. It was evident from an early age that he was the child chosen to be the one in the family who would be committed to education.

The family did all they could to make it possible for young Edward to excel. While they were not well off, their belief in education was rich. They recognized in their son the intellect, talent, drive, and ability to succeed. He excelled in academics and sports at Stanton High School and was valedictorian of his graduating class in 1915.

In the February 2002 issue of the magazine *BU Bridge*, Amy Dean, in a tribute to Gourdin, wrote that his son, Edward Jr., who passed away in 2013, recalled that his father's family "was a big supporter of academics. Often times in big, poor families, they'd pick one to be the pioneer." On winter days, he said, his father would "stuff newspapers in his shoes to keep warm while walking to his classes at Harvard. That was him."

His parents, wanting the best for their son, supported him when he left Jacksonville for Cambridge, Massachusetts, after high school, arranging for him to attend the legendary Cambridge High and Latin Preparatory School. After two years there, he entered Harvard in 1917 with the idea of playing baseball and then pursuing a law degree.

His freshman college diary provided a glimpse of the level of detail and discipline in this young man's makeup. On a website dedicated to Gourdin, www.EO Gourdin.com, developed by his relative Bill Tatum, it talks about the discipline young Gourdin showed as a freshman at Harvard. "First week of school, he marked down a payment of $50, the first installment of his $150 tuition fee. A few days later, he listed his class schedule for the first day of classes and reminded himself, 'Take the first weeks reading and map study for Monday.'"

However, he made his lasting mark in athletics, lettering in baseball, basketball, and track. Gourdin ran for Harvard during the school year and in the summer for the racially integrated Dorchester Athletic Club of Boston, which had been formed by middle-class African Americans.

Boston played a major role in Black cultural expression during the Harlem Renaissance of the 1920s and 1930s. The city by that time had an educated Black elite class—sometimes referred to as the Black Brahmins, after the Boston Brahmins—who laid the foundation for insistence on racial equality. In theater, dance, and literature, the community shined. In 1900, Booker T. Washington founded the National Negro Business League in Boston.

Its mission was "to bring the colored people who are engaged in business together for consultation, and to secure information and inspiration from each other." In 1910, the Eureka Co-Operative Bank in Boston opened, described by Jim Vrabel in his 2004 book, *When in Boston: A Time Line & Almanac*, as "the only bank in the East owned and operated by Colored People."

Meanwhile, Edward Gourdin distinguished himself in track. He was the National Amateur Athletic Union's junior 100-yard dash champion and the national pentathlon champion in 1921 and 1922. Yet it is for the long jump against the two elite British schools on that July day in 1921 in Cambridge that Gourdin, who was nicknamed "Ned," is immortalized in track and field records.

In 1924, after completing his law exams at Harvard, Gourdin traveled to Paris for the Olympics as the favorite not only to win the broad jump, but also to set a new world record. Although Gourdin had previously cleared twenty-five feet, his longest jump at the Paris Games was only 23'10", giving him second place behind fellow American William DeHart Hubbard, whose jump of 24'5" earned him the gold.

Ironically, Gourdin accomplished a long jump of 25'8" at an exhibition the day after the Olympic final. But it never counted as a world record because the jump occurred at a nonsanctioned event.

Gourdin won the silver medal behind Hubbard, the first African American to win an Olympic gold medal in an individual event. Hubbard, an outstanding athlete, would go on to set a long-jump world record of 25'10¾" at Chicago in June 1925, and he equaled the world record of 9.6 seconds for the 100-yard dash in his hometown of Cincinnati a year later.

But other accomplishments at the 1924 Olympics overshadowed Gourdin's silver medal win. Paavo Nurmi, the "Flying Finn," wowed the crowd by winning five gold medals in seven races in six days. Johnny Weissmuller of the United States, who would later become Hollywood's most famous Tarzan, took home three swimming gold medals. And British sprint champion Harold Abrahams, whom Gourdin had beat in the long jump and in the 100-yard run in 1921, won the 100 meters.

Dean's article also references Gourdin's roots in the context of where and when he grew up. "Considering the lack of probable opportunities a Black man had back then," says John Tenbroeck, a Jacksonville track and field historian, "his achievements are even more noteworthy. He obviously used his talents to the fullest extent."

America in 1924 was more than just the Roaring Twenties, a decade of prosperity and libertines, jazz bands and bootleggers. It was also the heyday of the resurgent Ku Klux Klan, and it was not just in the southern states that the Klan was a presence. Missing commencement week at Harvard spared Ned the sight of his well-heeled white classmates celebrating their third reunion by strutting about in Ku Klux Klan outfits, complete with white robes and peaked hats.

In 1923, Gourdin married Amalia Ponce of Cambridge; they would raise three daughters and a son. They met after a Harvard track meet. Many years later, wrote Dean in the *BU Bridge*, Amalia fondly recalled the day they met.

"I went to watch the meet with two or three girls," she remembered. "We saw Ned win and set the world record, and everyone in the crowd was jubilant. He was proud of his accomplishment but struck me as being very shy and mostly interested in his academics. You could tell he put his whole heart into all his efforts. And right there, I knew he would accomplish great things."

To make ends meet, Gourdin went to work as a postal clerk while in law school; he kept that job as he strove to establish his practice, finally resigning in 1927, citing the toll on his health. He wrote to a friend at the time, mixing in humor with ironic optimism.

"I am still in Cambridge, and still engaged in the great all-American game of chasing the dollar," Daphne Abeel chronicled in her 1997 piece, "Edward Gourdin, Brief Life of a Breaker of Barriers," for *Harvard Magazine*. "Although I was a sprinter in college, I seem to be a marathoner now. Still on the first million."

Gourdin was admitted to the Massachusetts bar in 1925 and to the federal bar in 1929. No law firm offered him a position; at that time there were few lawyers of color anywhere. Even a Harvard degree could not land him a position with a firm. He kept his job as a postal clerk, one he had worked while attending law school as he struggled to establish a law practice. During this period, his attention turned to the public sector. He became active in politics, originally as a Republican.

His conversion to the Democratic Party in the early 1930s led to relationships with political figures and attorneys in Boston, including Francis Ford, an influential lawyer whose classmate, Franklin Delano Roosevelt, had named him U.S. attorney for the district of Massachusetts in 1933. In 1936, with Ford's backing, Roosevelt appointed Gourdin assistant U.S. attorney, a position he would occupy, with the exception of the war years, until 1951.

Gourdin had joined the Student Training Corps as a sophomore at Harvard and enlisted in the National Guard in 1925. In 1941 he was assigned to the 372d Infantry, a segregated regiment, and became its commanding officer. In 1942 he was appointed colonel, seeing action in the South Pacific.

With a historic nod to the legendary all-Black Massachusetts 52nd Regiment that served heroically during the Civil War, the 372nd was a proud regiment with a history dating back to 1864. It served with distinction in the Spanish-American War and World War I.

For bravery in the battles of Meuse-Argonne and Alsace and Lorraine in 1918 in the last weeks of the Great War, the entire regiment was decorated with the Croix-de-Guerre with palm, a military medal commonly bestowed on foreign military forces allied to France, issued to units whose members performed heroic deeds in combat.

A decorated soldier, he was appalled at the racial separation in the military. Abeel also described Gourdin's frustrations with the racial politics of the military during his time. In his 1945 diary, he wrote, "We have been plagued for five years with newcomers (reserve officers and graduates of OCS) who seem to assume that Negro soldiers do not know anything." He rejoined the National Guard after his discharge in 1947, retiring in 1959 with the rank of brigadier general.

Back in Boston, he resumed his duties as assistant U.S. attorney and was promoted to chief of the civil division before his elevation to the bench in 1951 in the Roxbury District Court. Preserved in the private papers of Gourdin is an editorial from the *Boston Herald* in 1951 that wrote of his appointment: "The day may come when the fact that a new state appointment is a Negro will cease to be a matter of note. Unfortunately, that is not yet."

On the day in 1958 that Gourdin was sworn in as the first African American on the Massachusetts Superior Court, future Supreme Court justice Thurgood Marshall said, "This swearing-in is doubly important. First, because it is the first of its kind in New England, and second, because it represents another step along the road of justice rendered without regard for race or color."

During the civil rights era, Gourdin made a conscious choice to maintain his judicial neutrality, but he remained active in the Black community. His interests included the NAACP, the Roxbury Youth Program, and the New England Olympians.

Edward Gourdin passed away in 1966. He was eulogized as a "scholar, athlete, soldier, judge" on Law Day, May 1, 1997, when, through the efforts of his family and friends, people filled the marble hall of Old Suffolk County Courthouse to celebrate the unveiling of his portrait.

Edward Jr. lobbied for his late father to be honored by having his portrait hung at the Boston courthouse. He was also proud of his father's athletic accomplishments. In the *BU Bridge*, Dean quoted Edward Gourdin Jr. talking about how his father's athletic skills did not diminish as he got older:

"When I was in junior high," he said, "I ran the 60-yard dash, and my father was a great supporter. He taught me a lot and was always at the stadium to watch me. I remember kidding around with him one day in 1960 about racing him. He was sixty-three at the time, and I was in my mid-twenties. We had a dirt road beside our house, probably 150 yards long, and we raced for real. I took off and got a lead on him for the first twenty-five yards before he whistled by me like I was standing still. I was shocked. The man was still very fast."

In August 1997, appeals court justice Roderick Ireland, an African American, was appointed to the Massachusetts Supreme Judicial Court; again a "first Black" made headlines. This excerpt is from the *Harvard Magazine* piece, quoting superior court chief justice Joseph Tauro honoring Judge Gourdin:

"Judge Gourdin was a scholar of the law, a courteous and thoughtful judge, dedicated to his work on the bench, a true gentleman beloved by all his colleagues. His whole career was an example of the opportunity for public service," recalled Tauro that day at the ceremony.

In the 1920s, as a track star during his years at Harvard, and later in the 1950s with his appointment as judge of the Massachusetts Superior Court, Edward Gourdin proudly stood tall in the light of history. He lived a remarkably full life, as an athlete, scholar, lawyer, jurist, soldier, and family man.

Edward Gourdin's life of accomplishment and of breaking color barriers wasn't well known until the Jacksonville, Florida, *Times-Union* ranked the one hundred greatest Jacksonville-area athletes of the twentieth century in 1999. Gourdin's achievements were uncovered to reveal a "hidden treasure." In 2004, he was inducted into the African American Ethnic Sports Hall of Fame.

"For a kid who grew up in an impoverished family on Davis Street in Jacksonville," wrote Gene Frenette in the *Times-Union*, "he sure went far—and not just in the long jump."

A true Renaissance man, Edward "Ned" Gourdin sprinted, leaped, and lived a remarkably full life, one of public service, and will be forever remembered as a trailblazer.

15

The Latin Legend Who Broke the Seal

Emilio Navarro

In June 2008, Major League Baseball conducted a ceremonial draft to honor living ex-players from the Negro Leagues. The New York Yankees selected Emilio "Millito" Navarro, the Puerto Rican legend, who played for the New York Cuban Stars in the Negro Leagues from 1928 to 1929. He was 103. They honored him on September 18 by flying him in from Puerto Rico for a ceremony prior to their game against the Chicago White Sox.

Millito posed for photos with two Puerto Rican stars, Jorge Posada and Iván Rodríguez. He stood on the mound at Yankee Stadium and threw out the ceremonial first pitch. His toss reached catcher Jorge Posada on the fly from thirty feet away. He impressed the Yankee players with his physical dexterity. Author Lew Freedman, in his book *Latino Baseball Legends: An Encyclopedia*, wrote about what happened that day. "I mean, 103, that's ridiculous," said baseball star Alex Rodriguez, whose parents immigrated to New York City from the Dominican Republic. "He was doing push-ups a few minutes ago." Millito was astounded by the homage the Yankees made. "This is a dream for me," Navarro said. "I think I am in heaven."

But what most people don't know is that Emilio Navarro was so much more than a ballplayer who lived to a wonderful old age, surrounded by friends and family in his hometown of Ponce. He was a pioneer of baseball, not only in his town but in all of Puerto Rico; a teacher; an innovator in the educational world and mentor to thousands of children; and an inspiration to sports fans everywhere.

Emilio Navarro. The pride of the island.
African American Ethnic Sports Hall of Fame

Emilio "Millito" Navarro was born September 26, 1905, in Patillas, Puerto Rico, and was raised in the city of Ponce. His father was a shoemaker who died when Emilio was six, and his mother soon moved to Ponce where she had family.

He attended public school and found time to learn how to play baseball, and he loved it from the day he picked up a ball. At the age of eight, Millito learned the fundamentals of baseball from an older friend and was immediately smitten with the game. His first recollection of seeing a pro game happened at about this time. "The first professionals that I saw were a team of Puerto Ricans," he said.

From the age of twelve, Millito pitched in to help his family by working at odd jobs like selling peanuts, delivering newspapers, and shining shoes. In a piece for the Society for American Baseball Research (SABR), Joseph Gerard looked back at the early days of Emilio Navarro. "I worked a lot," Navarro said. He attended school in Ponce, and he loved to watch its baseball team play. "The school I attended used to compete with other schools, but I had no money so I used to sneak in. The team's coach asked me to replace a player. I got two hits, stole second base and then third. They put me on the team and I was given a uniform. It was a thrill," he said.

Navarro, an exceptionally fast runner, was a track star in high school, setting records in the long jump and hurdles. He was offered a track scholarship to attend college at the University of Puerto Rico in Mayagüez. But baseball was his first love. He began to play semiprofessionally in 1922, at the age of seventeen, for the Ponce Leones. He played games on weekends and was paid $25 per week. The money also played a role in his decision to forgo college; it was more important to help his mother financially.

Emilio Navarro became one of the all-time greats, and later a patriarch of baseball in Puerto Rico. Although standing only 5'5" and weighing only 160 pounds, he was renowned for his quick bat, blazing speed, great glove, strong arm, and soft hands. He developed into a gifted ballplayer and firmly believed that someday he would be ready to play in the major leagues in the United States.

In 1928, after six years with the Ponce team, Navarro was approached by a teammate who had been offered a contract to play for the great Cuban Stars of the Eastern Negro League. He traveled to New York in order to try out. Despite having no promise of a contract, Millito was confident enough in his abilities to take the trip to see how he'd do. In his book *Early Latino Players in the United States*, Nick Wilson wrote about Millito's first trip to the Big Apple. Upon arriving in the city, Navarro said, "Those high buildings all around—I imagined I was in heaven."

Navarro made the Stars roster in 1928, with a salary of $100 per month, and became the first Puerto Rican to play in the American Negro Leagues. In 1928, the Stars played in the Eastern Colored League, which was struggling before finally disbanding altogether in June. Navarro had eighty-four plate appearances and batted .229.

But in 1929 he found his stride, hitting .337, third best on the team. It was a high-scoring league; five hitters finished over .400. But the experience was bittersweet for Navarro, especially when they played in the South, where he felt discriminated against due to both his skin color and his lack of English.

Navarro's salary was increased to $125 a month. But, as Gerard tells in his SABR article, after two years of dealing with the harsh realities of race on the mainland in the late 1920s, as well as the language barrier, Navarro was eager to return to Puerto Rico. In the summer of 1929, the Stars joined four other teams from their former league, and the previously independent Homestead Grays also came aboard to form the new American Negro League. Soon afterward the league collapsed, and the Stars became an independent team.

In September 1933, Navarro traveled with the Ponce club to the Dominican Republic for a series of games against a powerful team from Venezuela that featured Josh Gibson and Luis Aparicio Sr. The Leones team stunned the visitors by winning both games of a doubleheader. Navarro then returned to Puerto Rico where he helped the Ponce Leones form a semipro league.

The experience and knowledge he acquired during these years contributed to his success when he became one of the founders of the Leones de Ponce baseball team in his hometown. He played, coached, and contributed in various other ways to the team, dedicating twenty years of his life to the Leones.

Navarro was still one of the finest infielders in the league into the early 1940s, when a knee injury forced him to the outfield. He also briefly served as the manager. In the 1940–1941 season, Navarro hit .311, and the following year he led his team to a 30-13 finish and the league championship.

Navarro retired as a player before the 1942–1943 campaign but served as a coach. The 1943–1944 Ponce Leones were one of the greatest Puerto Rican teams of all time, compiling a record of 37-7 and winning the championship. After four years as a coach with the Leones, Navarro retired from baseball and spent the next ten years serving as administrator of their home park, Montaner Stadium.

Following his career, Millito wanted to give something back to his community, so he devoted the next chapter of his life to working with young people. Navarro served as an athletic instructor and coach for the public school system in Ponce from 1935 until 1944. He worked in all twenty schools in the city, visiting at least four each day, and was responsible for developing the physical education program in his city. Due to the lack of space in the city schools, Millito developed programs to enhance physical coordination and endurance, such as running in circles, tug of war, short relays, and basic calisthenics, that could be carried out in confined spaces.

At that time in Ponce, there was no basketball, volleyball, or baseball because of the lack of facilities. Millito added these sports as after-school activities that would take place at the Charles H. Terry Stadium in Ponce. During his years as a teacher and coach, Navarro fielded many quality teams for the city and the Ponce high schools. His teams were particularly strong in baseball, basketball, and track.

Later, he opened a sporting goods store, and after that a gaming machine company named Shuffle Alley that was managed by his sons. Even at the age of 104, Millito was still putting in thirty hours a week at work. In the periodical *Latina Lista News from the Latinx Perspective*, Martha Alonso Hernandez said, "In 2005, at the age of 100, he was honored as 'America's Outstanding Oldest Worker.'"

Navarro's legacy as a player has been impacted by the circumstances of his career. He played much of his first six years as a professional in Venezuela, where records from that time are virtually nonexistent, and spent only two seasons, at ages twenty-three and twenty-four, in the American Negro Leagues. He finished his career in Puerto Rico with a batting average of .272.

Navarro married María Teresa Torres in 1935. Their marriage lasted fifty-one years until she died in 1986. They had four children. "He was an exquisite and excellent father," said his son Eric when he spoke to the Associated Press for his father's obituary. "He instilled us with honesty and above all respect for everybody."

In 2000, at the age of ninety-five, looking back on a life dedicated to excellence on the playing field and service to his community, Millito said, "God has been very good with me, giving me good and physical health. Ironically now, I'm just enjoying my youth in my latter years."

And, in a crowning achievement, Millito was inducted into the African American Ethnic Sports Hall of Fame in Guaynabo, Puerto Rico, on September 26, 2005, his one hundredth birthday.

Puerto Ricans often proudly identify themselves as Boricua, derived from the Taíno word *Boriken*, to illustrate their recognition of the island's indigenous Taíno heritage. The word translates to "land of brave lords." During the recognition ceremony at the Museo del Deporte (Museum of Sports) of Puerto Rico in commemoration of his century of life, Boricua player Emilio Navarro expressed himself eloquently. His words that day were printed in the *African American Sports Magazine*.

"Today it rains because God is crying. This is a happy moment, everyone is happy, and Millito is the happiest even when he is the oldest." The ceremony featured students from the Ponce School where Navarro studied his first years, who gave him a gift congratulating him on his birthday. Hundreds of sports personalities, politicians, former athletes, and his large extended family came together to congratulate the first Puerto Rican to play in the Negro Leagues.

Arif Khatib, president of the African American Ethnic Sports Hall of Fame, handed Millito a trophy that symbolized his induction. It was the first of many he received that day. The museum then announced the Emilio "Millito" Navarro Award, which will be awarded every year on the birthday of this revered baseball figure. The next day, the city of Ponce expressed their appreciation and honored him for his lifetime of service to Puerto Rico.

Navarro was inducted into the Puerto Rican Sports Hall of Fame in 1953 and elected to the Puerto Rico Baseball Hall of Fame in 1992 and the Hispanic Heritage Baseball Museum in 2006. He was known for his cheerful nature and dapper dress. In an August 2010 interview with the Associated Press, he said he did not have any secrets to a long life but that he enjoyed dancing and the occasional glass of whiskey.

On April 27, 2011, he had a minor heart attack, and on April 30 he suffered a stroke and died soon afterward, surrounded by his family. Survivors include his four children, eleven grandchildren, nine great-grandchildren, and one great-great-grandchild. He is buried in the Cementerio La Piedad in Ponce.

"He was a stellar baseball player in Latin America for the Negro Leagues," said baseball historian Luis R. Mayoral, who was quoted in the SABR piece. "And in Puerto Rico, he was highly respected in relation to the game of baseball." At the time of his death, at age 105, he was the oldest former professional baseball player and the last surviving player from the American Negro League.

Emilio "Millito" Navarro left a rich legacy, not the least part of which was his abiding love for baseball and the rewarding life it afforded him. "When I played, I met many people who loved me for my whole life," he said in Freedman's book. "So even though I didn't have much money, I was always happy."

16

Breaking Records across the Pacific

Chi Cheng

Chi Cheng is the greatest Asian female sprinter of all time. She held seven world records at once. Her 100-yard record set in 1970 lasted almost forty years. She also won seventy-seven gold medals in international competitions. In the 1968 Olympics in Mexico City, she won the bronze medal in the 80-meter hurdles. In 1970, she set five world outdoor records.

During the 1969–1970 season, out of 154 events (sprints, hurdles, long jump, and relays) entered, she only lost once. She was expected by coaches, writers, journalists, commentators, and fans to win at least one gold medal at the 1972 Olympics in Munich. But she could not compete due to injury and was forced to retire early.

Her triumphs on the track brought her many awards and honors. She was named Athlete of the Year by the track and field world and at the same time was chosen as Global Athlete of the Year by the Associated Press. In 2000, Chi Cheng was voted Female Asian Athlete of the Twentieth Century by the Asian Athletics Association. Yet no one outside her native Taiwan knows about her amazing athletic accomplishments.

The word *Formosa* means "beautiful isle" in Portuguese. That name was first recorded during the age of exploration by a Portuguese ship that sailed past the island in 1542, and it remained the primary name for Taiwan in the West until 1949. The island became a Japanese colony in 1895. Taiwan exported sugar and rice to Japan and developed its industry to feed the needs of the growing Japanese military. When the war between Japan and China broke out in 1937, Taiwanese men were "encouraged" to enlist in the Japanese military; over thirty thousand were killed during the war.

During the war years, brutal punishment was administered for any sign of disobedience. Many Taiwanese women were recruited as "comfort women" during the

Chi Cheng. The will to win.
Courtesy of Chi Cheng

war, which still causes political tension between the Republic of China (Taiwan) and Japan today.

At the beginning of the war, missions against British Malaya and the Philippines were launched from Taiwan. Japanese airfields on the island were bombed during the American invasion of the Philippines and Okinawa. In 1949, Taiwan formally became known as the Republic of China. Under the leadership of Chinese revolutionary military leader Chiang Kai-shek, who passed away in 1975, they became a strong, sovereign country.

Now fast-forward to 1960. A young Taiwanese girl, only sixteen, is in the 1960 Rome Olympics running the 80-meter hurdles, one of only three women representing her home country. She does not earn a medal but acquits herself well at the Games, absorbing tips and learning the ropes of big-time track and field. And she pays attention, whetting her appetite for more competition.

While competing in Rome, she gets noticed by an American track and field collegiate coach who is assigned by the State Department to coach the Indian team. They meet again two years later when the man, this time as the coach of the Nationalist China track team, sees her run at the provincial games in Taiwan where she breaks four national records—in the 80-meter hurdles, the high jump, the long jump, and the pentathlon.

Impressed, he writes a letter to her government in which he says that she needs to be in the United States to receive better training. The government pays for a scholarship to college, and he convinces her to come to America to train with him. As a young man, he had been quite the sprinter and hurdler himself, and in this tall, determined Taiwanese girl he sees a special quality that he had recognized in the greats he had observed throughout the years, and in some cases had coached.

She was as fast as the wind, and she could jump. But what set her apart was her determination to be the best. Although modest and retiring in nature, when she hit the blocks she became a tiger. And within a few months she had taken the track world by storm, along the way becoming one of the all-time greats.

"I was sent to the States," Chi recalled, quoted by Rohit Brijnath in his piece "50 Years Ago, World's Fastest Woman Was an Asian" that appeared in the *Straits Times* in July 2020, "and I knew my responsibility was to follow C. K. Yang's footsteps to get a medal in the Olympics. When I won bronze, I felt I had done my duty. For me it was such a relief. After that medal I started to enjoy competition. There is such a difference in the psychological state of mind. And all of a sudden I started breaking world records."

Chi Cheng was born in Hsinchu, Taiwan, a large coastal city on the northern coast of the island. It was 1944, and World War II was raging. Taiwan was cast in its net. She was the third of seven children in a poor family. Two younger sisters were adopted when they were small. Her father, a grocer, left the family when she was twelve.

Her earliest years were a time of moving from one cheap rented house to another. She was always devoted to her mother, and they endured a life of hardship until she was fourteen. She did well in school, enjoyed literature, and hoped to go to the Normal University in Taipei; her aim was to become a teacher.

Always fast in the children's games that were played in nearby rice paddies and in provincial races, she showed great skill as a sprinter. It was in junior high school that her talent became apparent to those around her. After she had begun to train seriously, Vincent Reel, the American collegiate track and field coach who had discovered Chi's talent in Rome and later in Taiwan, wrote letters to officials praising her world-class potential.

In 1962, Chi, eighteen, got a five-year full scholarship to attend California State Polytechnic University in Pomona. Reel was the track coach at nearby Claremont College and became her personal coach. She went to America to follow in the footsteps of countryman C. K. Yang, her inspiration who'd won the silver medal in the decathlon at Rome in the 1960 Olympics. Yang went on to set the world record in April 1963 and was on the cover that year of *Sports Illustrated* under the headline "World's Best Athlete."

Later that year, she went back home and won the women's pentathlon title in Taiwan Province. Chi would always have the fastest speed in the 80-meter hurdles field, but her height was a disadvantage. Brijnath, in his piece in the *Straits Times*, quoted Chi: "I was the tallest among the medalists and penalized for my height. Every hurdle I had to chop my steps. After the Mexico City Games in 1968 they changed to the 100m for women's hurdles and between the hurdles there was more distance, which was much better for me."

Later that year, Reel thought it would be a good idea for Chi to transfer to the University of Hawaii and run for their women's track club. There she met lifetime friend and fellow champion runner Lacey O'Neal, who was also attending college there. O'Neal grew up in Chicago, blossomed as a hurdler at the University of Hawaii, and in 1973 traveled the world as a professional runner with the International Track Association. Lacey discussed her over half century of friendship with Cheng and what that means to her.

"I called Chi my 'little sister,' even though we were the same age," O'Neal recalled fondly. "In Hawaii, we were roommates, both of us on scholarship. I was responsible for her. Coach Reel thought that Chi would thrive in Hawaii, with its large Asian population and beautiful weather. We trained together—she was a determined athlete. She was tall, beautiful, and a sweet person. And she was a prodigy on the track. The USA gave her the opportunity to be a great athlete," O'Neal said, "and those who ran against her got better."

When she moved to California in 1963 to be trained by Coach Reel, he thought Chi could become a world-class athlete. In an interview with former track star Rosie Bonds, Bonds shared a story about when she and Chi were young runners competing against each other. "Chi told Vincent she wanted to be as good as me because I beat her," said Bonds. "He told her, 'You should not want to be as good as anyone else. You are the best.' She told him that I was better than her, and he finally accepted that."

"I ran against Chi, and she beat me in our very first race," said Bonds. "I vowed at that moment to never come in second again. And I thank her for helping me become a more committed runner. She was determined, challenging, and an excellent competitor. I found her to be a very nice person," said Bonds, an Olympic hurdler herself.

Chi participated in the '60, '64, and '68 Olympics in the 80-yard hurdles. She described a story of failure from her first Olympics in 1960 and how it motivated her to press harder. "I was only 16, and I came last in my heat in the 80m hurdles. I didn't quit, and if I wasn't last in my heat I wouldn't have won bronze in 1968," Chi said in the *Straits Times* piece. She went on, "As an Asian, I attracted attention. They were curious that this yellow-skinned Asian girl was able to run so fast."

International and comparative education scholar Minju Choi of Stanford described the narrow prism through which Asian American history is taught in U.S. schools. "As more states include Asian American history in their curriculums, the question of what and how we are going to teach that history remains," Choi said in a February 2022 piece in the *San Francisco Chronicle* titled "Anti-Asian Hate Is Still on the Rise. Ending It Has to Start in the Classroom."

Many people are appalled by the emergence of racism directed at Asian Americans and the dramatic increase in hate crimes today. It is long past time to end this pointless prejudice, but we find ourselves in the same vicious cycle. Some major event, like 9/11 or the coronavirus, happens, and all too often Americans are looking at "the other," namely a dark-skinned ethnic group, to scapegoat and punish.

In view of the current climate with Asian American hate crimes on the rise, one can only imagine what it was like for an Asian American track and field star to run in America during the 1960s. That question was asked of Chi in 1968 while participating in the 1968 Olympics in Mexico City.

She was well aware of the protest for human rights at the Games with Dr. John Carlos and Dr. Tommie Smith. "I felt bad about the athletes having to raise their fists in protest of racism, and I agreed with them," she told O'Neal. "Although I was not treated the way African Americans were in America, I totally supported them all the way."

O'Neal continued, "Chi competed against several American Olympians and told me she was too busy trying to win to think about racism."

It was difficult in the 1950s and 1960s, Lacey O'Neal remembered. "I always felt a disadvantage being Black and female," she said. O'Neal later traveled with other athletes and public figures as part of Operation Champ, a government-sponsored initiative to help promote fellowship between Blacks and whites in riot-torn southern cities.

In 1964, Chi made the Olympic team representing Taiwan. That summer in the Tokyo Olympics, while running hard against the Russian star Galina Bystrova, Chi hit a hurdle and injured her thigh. The injury kept her from further competition and ended her running for the year.

Cheng sustained other injuries; she had surgery on her knee in 1967 and pulled muscles in both legs in 1968, but she was perseverant and continued her training. At the 1968 Olympics in Mexico City, she placed third in the 80-meter hurdles and seventh in the 100-meter run. By 1969, her legs had healed and her speed was back—and then some. Chi was so dominant that in the 1969–1970 season, she only lost one race out of 154 events.

Over time, Cheng and Reel, who himself had been an outstanding collegiate sprinter and hurdler at Long Beach City College and Occidental College, developed a strong personal as well as professional bond. In 1970, after eight years of working together, they got married in Taipei. Later they had a daughter, who was born in Taiwan. But the child, being of mixed race, was not totally accepted in Taiwanese society, and Chi decided to bring her back to the United States to live with Reel, from whom she had separated. Later, back in Taiwan, she remarried and had a second child.

At the February 1970 AAU meet at Madison Square Garden, she won the long jump, the 60-yard hurdles, and the 60-yard dash. Chi, who that day proudly wore the flag of the Republic of China—"blue sky, white sun, and a wholly red earth"—on her uniform, bowed graciously and shed tears. She was thinking, she said later, of her mother, who supported the family as a washerwoman, and of her home country, which made it possible for her to go to the United States for the coaching that made her a world champion.

In June 1970, Cheng set world records in the 100 yards, 100 meters, 220 yards, and 200 meters at the Rose Festival in Portland, Oregon. She clocked 10.0 seconds for the first "even time" ever in the 100-yard dash. Between Portland, Los Angeles, Munich, and Vienna that year, she broke or equaled seven world records and lost only one race. *Time* magazine ran a story on her, calling her the "Taiwan Flash." Her countrymen nicknamed her "Iron Girl," while the Japanese called her the "Flying Antelope" because she could leap as well as run.

"Those were really great days," Chi said, from the *Straits Times* article. "Heide Rosendahl [the German long jumper who won gold and silver medals in Munich] approached me in Munich and said you broke the world record in the 100-meter hurdles. I jumped up and down in happiness and stepped on her foot with my spikes!"

In the eighty-nine-year history of the AP Woman Athlete of the Year Award, only two Asians have won the award: U.S. Open champion golfer Se-ri Pak in 1998 and Chi Cheng in 1970. When asked what it felt like to be the fastest woman in the world, she said in the same article, "It didn't affect my life much. . . . It was nice to be honored. But I was still very much Chi Cheng."

In December 1970, a knee injury, coupled with a severe hip injury, removed her from competition. Her pain made even walking difficult. Returning to Taiwan for surgery in April 1972 to remove a muscle in her left thigh, she spent fifty-two days in the hospital.

When she returned to America, her running days were over; she first had to learn to walk. Once recovered, Chi became the women's athletic director and the track coach at Redlands University, working with Reel. No one thought she would be unable to compete in the Olympic Games that summer in Munich.

She worked incessantly to get back in shape and returned as an alternate for Taiwan in the 1972 Munich Games. In 1973, she traveled the world, competing with the International Track Association. She would go on to coach track at the University of Florida. Later she worked for the State Department supporting the U.S. embassies in the Ivory Coast and Burkina Faso, then joined the Peace Corps and worked in Gambia.

In 1977, Chi Cheng returned to Taiwan and held the post of director general of the National Track and Field Association, and in 1987 she received a special medal from the International Amateur Athletic Union. From 1981 to 1990, Chi Cheng served on the first legislature of the Republic of China under President Ma Ying-jeou.

In 1992 she launched the annual Long-Distance Run for the Chinese People's Health and Vitality. Since then, there have been tens of thousands of participants. Ms. Cheng also served as the national policy advisor in 2010 and 2011. In 2001 she was elected to the International Scholar-Athlete Hall of Fame.

In 2003, Chi published her autobiography. She currently serves as the honorary chairman of the Chinese Taipei Track and Field Association and as a member of the Chinese Taipei Olympic Committee. In recent years, Chi Cheng has worked to advocate for sports exchanges and cooperation across the Taiwan Strait with mainland China.

But she will always be remembered for her dominance on the track and her humble, gentle demeanor off of it.

17

From the Football Field to the Battlefield

Eugene Evans and Eli Page Howard

"For years on Memorial Day in Pelham, NY, just outside New York City, 65 names have been read of natives and residents who died in military service. Two of those names were best friends, African Americans, and outstanding athletes and marines. After the war both enrolled at Morgan State University in Baltimore and played on their national championship football team. Sadly, both died heroically in military service." These were the words of Ken Kraetzer, graduate of Pelham High School and Providence College, executive director of the Sons of the American Legion Radio, and broadcaster of West Point football for WVOX in New Rochelle, New York, in his 2011 piece for *Bleacher Report*, "Memorial Day: Remembering Two Army Veterans from Morgan State."

It is a tradition since the Civil War to place American flags on the grave sites of veterans on Memorial Day. The practice is followed every year, from Arlington National Cemetery where three hundred thousand flags will be placed, to veterans' cemeteries in every state and at smaller neighborhood burial sites across the country. In New Rochelle, New York, there is the grave site of Pelham native Eugene Lee Evans, who was a star college football player sixty years ago. And in Arlington National Cemetery, his teammate and friend Eli Page Howard is honored.

Eugene Evans and Eli Page Howard made the supreme sacrifice; they gave their lives for their country. In this chapter, we remember these two men, athletes who made their mark at a New York high school; then together competed at Morgan State University, one of the first historically Black colleges; and fought and died heroically overseas as soldiers in two different wars, far from home.

We felt it was important to include details of their respective sacrifices in this chapter so that we may understand exactly what they did. The field of battle is very

Lieutenant Eugene Evans. He gave his all for his country. *African American Ethnic Sports Hall of Fame*

different from the football field, but if you look, you can see similarities and connections. The leadership that both men showed as young athletes translated to becoming leaders in college and in the service.

Lieutenant Eugene Evans was a natural—charismatic, politically astute, and a leader—who volunteered for a dangerous mission in Korea in 1952. Colonel Eli Page Howard served several years in the military; he was forty-one and on his second tour of Vietnam when he was killed in action in 1969.

Evans, who was known as "Dippy," played on the CIAA national championship team of Morgan State in 1949, and then, as a young married army officer, died in combat in the Korean War just three years later.

Evans's teammate at Pelham Memorial High School just north of New York City and later in college at Morgan State, Howard was also an extraordinary athlete during the late 1940s. He had a long and distinguished military career. He served in Korea and returned to the battlefield in Vietnam, serving two combat tours there. He died serving our country as a U.S. Army officer on his second tour in Vietnam in 1969.

Eli Page Howard. Patriotism to the end.
African American Ethnic Sports Hall of Fame

The athletic exploits of these two young men from Pelham where they grew up is well known in the Pelham community, as is the heroism they displayed as army officers when faced with the extreme challenges of leading troops in combat.

In high school, Evans was an extraordinary athlete, probably the best in the history of Pelham High. He batted .444 for the baseball team, in basketball he was all-county, and in track he was a star high jumper. In football he was a three-year letterman, making the all-county and all-metropolitan New York area as an end. Evans was cocaptain of the undefeated 1945 Pelham team, which outscored its opponents 183–13.

On top of his athletic achievements, Evans was respected and popular and was elected to the student council as secretary of his graduating class. When he was inducted posthumously into the inaugural class of the Pelham Hall of Honor in 2009, a number of alumni of that era spoke fondly of their memories of him. Some of the old-timers mentioned that Evans was scouted by Major League Baseball teams. We will never know where his potential as an athlete or charismatic personality might have taken him.

Eli Page Howard, or Tim, as he was called growing up, was a year behind Evans in high school, where as quarterback he cocaptained the undefeated 1945 Pelham football team after Evans graduated. He was known as the "Touchdown King."

After graduation from Pelham, both Howard and Evans went on to serve in the Marine Corps during the postwar era, when African Americans still trained at different camps and served in segregated units. After their service in the marines, both enrolled at Morgan State College in Baltimore. The football team was led by the legendary coach Eddie Hurt, who was in the middle of compiling a 173-54-18 record at the school with fourteen CIAA conference titles. Two players of that era at Morgan, Len Ford and Roosevelt Brown, were elected into the NFL Hall of Fame.

From 1932 to 1939, Hurt's football teams played fifty-four games without defeat, one of the longest unbroken strings on record. Hurt also coached Morgan State basketball from 1929 to 1947. During his tenure, the basketball team won CIAA titles in three successive years: 1931, 1932, and 1933. In track and field, his teams won eighteen track and field championships after entering the conference in 1930. Hurt will go down in history as the greatest coach ever to come from a Black college. He was honored posthumously with the 2011 AFCA Trailblazer Award, created to honor those who coached at historically Black colleges and universities.

"The arrival of the Black athlete on the national sports scene in the 1940s and 1950s goes directly back to Edward P. Hurt," wrote Herman L. Wade, Hurt's biographer in the book *Run from There: A Biography of Edward P. Hurt*. "There is not a single Black sports figure in the world today who is not in some small way in the debt of Coach Hurt. And to the extent that Hurt helped to break down racial barriers, our entire country owes him a huge debt of gratitude. We are a better nation because of him."

When asked about his success, Hurt's words were remembered by his alma mater on their hall of fame website: "If I've done anything at all, it's been because of other coaches," said Hurt. "The men, the colleges, the administration, the alumni, friends, just everybody. I've only had one formula, and that's hard work."

Perhaps for a moment we can remember those two young men as they were, star athletes playing for Morgan State College as it was known then. (It is now Morgan State University.) Evans and Howard led the Morgan State Bears to a CIAA title in 1949, which was considered the national championship of historical Black colleges. Howard was the quarterback and Evans a receiver on that undefeated 1949 team, one that outscored their opponents 227–33, the highlight of a November contest when they defeated archrival Wilberforce, 14–13, at the Polo Grounds in New York City. In 1974, Evans was named to the Morgan State Athletic Hall of Fame.

In addition to football, Evans and Howard were cadets in the brand-new Reserve Officer Training Corps program started at Morgan State in response to President

Harry Truman's 1948 Executive Order 9981, which directed that the military be integrated.

In 1940, African Americans made up almost 10 percent of the U.S. population. During World War II, the army had become the nation's largest minority employer. Of the 2.5 million African American males who registered for the draft through December 31, 1945, more than one million were inducted into the armed forces. Along with thousands of Black women, these inductees served in all the military branches during the war.

President Franklin Roosevelt, in the beginning of his unprecedented third term in office, had responded to complaints about discrimination at home against African Americans by issuing an executive order in June 1941 directing that Black Americans be accepted into job-training programs in defense plants. This order also forbade discrimination by defense contractors and established a Fair Employment Practices Commission.

In December 1946, President Harry Truman appointed a panel to serve as the President's Commission on Civil Rights, which recommended "more adequate means and procedures for the protection of the civil rights of the people of the United States."

When the commission issued its report in October 1947, among its proposals were anti-lynching and anti–poll tax laws and strengthening the civil rights division of the Department of Justice. Sadly, it took until 2022 for the anti-lynching law to finally get passed by the U.S. Senate.

In February 1948, Truman called on Congress to enact all of these recommendations. When southern senators threatened a filibuster, Truman used his executive powers; he bolstered the civil rights division, appointed the first African American judge to the federal bench, and named several other African Americans to high-ranking administration positions. And on July 26, 1948, he issued the historic executive order 9981, which abolished segregation in the armed forces and ordered full integration of all branches.

The order stated that "there shall be equality of treatment and opportunity for all persons in the armed forces without regard to race, color, religion, or national origin."

At Morgan State, Eli Howard excelled in military duties and was named the first "cadet commander" of the new ROTC program, which in years that followed would be known for producing generals.

Meanwhile, the affable Evans, ever the outgoing politician, served as a member of the student council at college, as commissioner of intramural athletics, and as the student representative to the college committee on intercollegiate athletics. In 1951, Evans went back to his alma mater in Pelham as a student teacher of physical education to finish out his senior year of college. Soon after graduation and commissioning as a second lieutenant in the army, Evans married Mildred Onley. Just a year later, Lieutenant Evans was sent to Korea, a member of the Thirty-Second Infantry Regiment, Seventh Infantry Division.

At the outset of the war in 1950, the division, originally made up of eighteen thousand soldiers, had been depleted to nine thousand men. To replenish the ranks of the understrength division, the Republic of Korea Army assigned 8,600 Korean soldiers to the division. Also fighting with the Seventh Infantry Division were members of the three battalions sent by Emperor Haile Selassie of Ethiopia as part of the UN forces.

On the night of July 19, 1952, Lieutenant Evans led a scout mission across enemy lines, testing enemy positions before an anticipated battle. The small group of soldiers was ambushed, one soldier was taken prisoner, and several escaped. Lieutenant Evans was killed.

The Seventh Infantry Division was awarded the Republic of Korea Presidential Unit Citation for "exceptional meritorious service to South Korea" for service at Inchon and during the entire Korean conflict, 1950–1953.

In 2009, a reception in honor of Eugene Evans's widow Mildred was arranged at the hospital where she had worked for years. The event was described by Kraetzerin's article. "Millie was well liked and respected by her coworkers. On why she had never remarried, her comment was, 'I never met anyone like my husband.'"

Eli Howard graduated from Morgan State in 1951 and in June entered the service as a second lieutenant. Howard served in Korea in 1952; returned to Fort Dix, New Jersey; and in 1957 went overseas to Germany. From June 1961 to February 1964, he was at the Armor School in Fort Knox, Kentucky. He served in Vietnam in 1964 as a senior advisor to the Army of the Republic of Vietnam.

Howard also served in Korea, later in Europe and Vietnam, and at the Pentagon in Washington, DC, rising to the level of lieutenant colonel. For his second tour in Vietnam, Colonel Howard was named commander of the Third Battalion of the 196th Light Infantry Brigade. On August 19, 1969, he was leading his unit from a helicopter during a fierce battle. The helicopter was shot down amid fighting so intense that American forces could not get to the crash site for five days. When they got there, they found no survivors.

Released by the U.S. Army on August 22, 1969—"U.S. Forces Blocked From Downed Copter":

"Saigon—North Vietnamese troops entrenched in bunkers kept up attacks today on American infantrymen trying to reach the wreckage of a helicopter southwest of Da Nang. A U.S. spokesman estimated that the lead column of 400 men from the 196th Light Infantry Brigade was about 800 yards from the site where the North Vietnamese shot down the helicopter.

"'Every time they start moving they draw fire,' said one U.S. officer. 'I've never seen the enemy fight so hard,' said another. 'Ordinarily they'll fight for a while and then pull back, but these guys are standing their ground and fighting.'

"Dive bombers and helicopter gunships made attack after attack on the North Vietnamese bunkers. For three days more than 1,000 North Vietnamese troops blocked American efforts to reach the crash site in the rolling foothills 31 miles southeast of Da Nang. Among the eight men aboard the helicopter was Colonel Eli P. Howard, Jr., a battalion commander. All eight men are believed dead."

An article from the *Standard Star*, New Rochelle, New York, August 29, 1969, read:

"Pelham—Funeral services for Lieutenant Colonel Eli Page Howard, former Pelham resident, who was killed August 19 in Vietnam, will take place Tuesday, September 2, at 10:45 a.m. at the Fort Myer Chapel, Arlington, Virginia. Colonel Howard will be interred in Arlington National Cemetery beside his father, a veteran of World War I who died in 1965. Colonel Howard, who was 41, lost his life along with seven others when a helicopter from which he was directing units of his command was brought down by enemy fire."

Colonel Howard was serving his second tour of duty in Vietnam and was commander of the Third Battalion of the 196th Light Infantry Brigade. After two years at the Department of the Army, in 1969 he volunteered for Vietnam duty and returned to combat, serving in the Mekong Delta. His career track was very similar to that of General Colin Powell; perhaps he would have made general one day.

In 2011, a soldier from the Third Infantry Division, known as the "Old Guard," placed a small flag at the Howards' grave site in preparation for Memorial Day. Colonel Howard's internment site is the last grave site at the top of Arlington's section 39. His wife, who raised their family alone after his death, is also interred at our nation's most hallowed grounds. You can find his name honored on the Vietnam Memorial Wall.

In 2007, at a ceremony in Harlem, both Lieutenant Evans and Colonel Howard were inducted into the African American Ethnic Sports Hall of Fame. Teammates on the field and heroes on the battlefield, theirs was the ultimate sacrifice.

18

Age Is Just a Number

Irene Obera

As an athlete, when do you have time to train and run when you are a high school principal? How do you dominate your age group in the master sprints for over forty-five years? How do you become an international star without becoming an Olympian? If you are Irene Obera, you start your track career when you are ready—and never stop running. Retirement means different things to different people. To Obera, eighty-nine, it meant hitting the gym, playing tennis, or bowling in a weekly league. Until recently, in a typical week, Irene did each of those activities several times.

"I enjoy competing, and you can't compete if you don't train," Obera said in a 2019 interview with Chris Stafford of WISP (Women in Sports). "My training has been spotty so far, but I know how it usually works. All of a sudden, 'Boom,' it comes back and my times drop. I'm still planning on winning, and I call winning first, not second."

Irene Obera has done a lot of winning. She is the reigning women's master sprinter in the United States. She has won so many races and meets it's hard to keep track of, and she holds several records for different age groups. She started out in her early twenties as a sprinter, with hopes of representing her country in the Olympics, and, in the middle of what would be a long, dedicated, and accomplished career as an educator, decided to take up "masters" running. And a master she became, and then some.

"Quitters never win, and winners never quit," so says the old sports adage. Irene Obera lives it. "They say you can't do this, you can't do that; it would motivate me more," she told Stafford in 2019. "I always have loved to challenge people; I don't think about age, like most people. I'd run against a 5-year-old or a 20-year-old. It doesn't matter. If you don't use it, you lose it."

Irene Obera. In the starting blocks.
African American Ethnic Sports Hall of Fame

Irene Romona Obera was born December 7, 1933, in San Bernardino County, California, and is a celebrated Filipina track and field athlete. She is the greatest woman master sprinter of all time. Over a long career, she has gathered quite a cache of achievements and records. She is a world-renowned member of the women's over-70 world record–holding 4×100-meter relay team. She also holds the current American record in the women's over-60 and over-75 100-meter run, and the women's over-75 200-meter run.

"My father was a boxer," Obera recalled in the WISP interview. "So he said when he had kids they would do sports. My older sister was my role model. She was very competitive at school and sports and played tennis at junior college." Softball was the first sport Irene got into; the guys would always have better facilities, but she loved the competition.

"Once you meet a goal, you just set another one and keep going," Obera continued. "The thing I've always enjoyed the most is the competition. I just want to do my best. I remember when I played softball sprinting toward home plate and taking out the catcher. They told me, 'You can't do that.' Well, that's how I was taught to play.

"I think it is important to remember that a young person's sports experience is about them and not about the parents," Obera continued. "Parents should have the goal of being as supportive of the child as possible."

Throughout her life, Obera has specialized in sprint events. Over her extended career she has set many world records and won numerous world championships. She was a winning machine well into her eighties. Her ability to win races is well documented. It was just a matter of time before she would be declared the greatest masters runner ever.

Obera was a relatively late entry into sports. She played field hockey, softball, and basketball while attending Chico State College. There was no track for women then. While most amateur athletes began to think of how to make money in their chosen sport, she did not give serious thought to participating in sports after graduation, but she was still fascinated with sports. She graduated from Chico State College with a teaching credential in 1957.

One summer during her college years, she tried out for a women's fast-pitch softball team that wound up playing a game against the Hollywood All-Stars, an outfit that included Frank Sinatra.

"I was at softball practice when a teammate told me she was a track champion," she recalled in her conversation with Stafford. "I thought to myself, 'If she is a champion, I know I can be one, too.' You might say I was a bit cocky."

Obera ran in her first meet in 1958 and made the national championships in 1959. She discovered it was fun, eventually running against the likes of Wilma Rudolph, who was the second African American to win an Olympic gold medal for the United States, Alice Coachman being the first.

She made the national championship team in 1959 and qualified for the 1960 U.S. Olympic trials, which were held at Stanford. She barely missed advancing to the 100-meter final, won by Rudolph. An injury sidelined her in 1964, but she qualified for the Olympic trials again in 1968, right before she turned thirty-five, and ran the 100 meters in 12.1 seconds in the semifinals.

"I knew I never wanted to run long distance—the shorter the better," she said to WISP.

"I competed against Irene while we were in thirteen California Nationals Girls Championships. Irene was a fantastic athlete. We also competed at the '60 Olympic trials in Texas. No one was more dedicated and determined," said Rosie Bonds, Olympic hurdler, sister of Bobby Bonds and aunt of Barry Bonds.

Obera was featured in *Sports Illustrated*'s "Faces in the Crowd" in the June 18, 1962, issue. It read, "Irene Obera, of Berkeley, California, has out-sprinted everyone on her home state tracks this season with three breezy 10.9s and an 11.0 in the 100-yard dash, and gives promise of being a front-runner for the AAU nationals next month in Los Angeles."

She was a pioneer in masters athletics, but it wasn't easy at first. In 1974, when she was forty-one, she suffered a bout of sarcoidosis, a disease characterized by the growth of inflammatory cells, usually in the lungs and lymph nodes, but it can also affect the eyes, skin, and heart. The cause is unknown, and there is no cure. Most people do well with no treatment, and in some cases sarcoidosis goes away on its own. However, it may last for years and can cause organ damage.

Irene's illness left her bedridden for most of the year. She heard about the first world masters championships due to be held in Toronto, Ontario, Canada, in 1975. She used that meet as a goal for her recovery. To her surprise, she didn't win there. It motivated her to return.

It wasn't until she reached the forty-five age group that she began to pile up world championship wins and records. As she passed through each age division, forty-five to seventy, she set the world record in the 200 meters. For the fifty, fifty-five, sixty, and sixty-five age groups, she won the 100 meters. In 2014, when she was eighty, she became the oldest woman to break forty seconds for the 200 meters, running 38.10 in a meet at UC Berkeley.

Obera had a long and rich career from 1958 to 1994 as an educator for the Berkeley Unified School District, starting out as a physical education teacher. Later she taught computer skills, playing a crucial role in the development of the computer lab in that era. She eventually became Berkeley's first female continuation school principal. She coached the girls' track team, and during her time in the district, Berkeley High School won the state girls' track team title in 1974, 1976, 1981, 1982, and 1983.

"I loved my experience in Berkeley," she said in the WISP interview. "I just had a great staff, and I enjoyed my time wherever I was in the district." The last eight years of her teaching career were at Willard Middle School, where she taught PE.

Thelette Bennett is a retired vice principal in the Berkeley Unified School District, and she and Irene Obera go way back.

"I have known Irene since I was eleven and she was about twenty-six. She used to come to San Pablo Park to play sports, and she became friends with my parents," Bennett said. "She was my PE teacher in middle school, and much later we were colleagues at Berkeley High and Willard. She was a terrific teacher—tougher than nails—you did not mess with Ms. Obera. When she just missed making the Olympics in 1960, it pushed her to become the athlete she became later.

"Irene was kind and encouraging. She was a mentor for me; I depended on her for guidance. Whenever anybody needed a resource to help them teach, she was there. She was professional—if she was gonna do something, she was gonna do it right," Bennett said.

As a woman of color who grew up in the 1950s in Texas, Bennett experienced plenty of discrimination. And although she never saw any directed at Obera, she knew that Irene had faced it too. "I am sure she had to experience some of that," Bennett said.

"What prepared me to teach were the people around me I learned from," said Bennett. "And I learned how to treat people from Irene. As a rookie administrator, she helped me a lot. She is dear to my heart. Irene was one of the earthly angels."

In 1996, Obera was elected into the inaugural class of the USATF Masters' Hall of Fame. After setting three world indoor records in the 60-, 200-, and 400-meter runs, Obera was named USATF Athlete of the Week for March 19, 2014. On July 12, 2014, at the San Francisco Track and Field Club's Pride Track & Field Meet in Hayward, California, Obera broke two world records in the 80- and 200-meter hurdles. These marks were her sixth and seventh world marks that year.

"I took up hurdling when I was 80—why not?" she said to Ken Stone of Masters track.com in the June 2018 issue. In 2018, Obera, then eighty-five, earned five gold medals at the WMA indoor championships in Torun, Poland, including eighty-five-and-over records in the 60 meters (12.28), the 200 meters (44.18), and the 4×200-meter relay (3:18.43). She has won twenty-four gold medals in the 100, 200, 400, and 4×400 relay events, setting numerous world age-group records.

"I remember Ms. Obera when I was a student at Berkeley. I was impressed with the fact that, unlike most athletes, she began to run much later in life. I remember she used to attend my basketball games when I played for Berkeley High. She was well respected, but I didn't get the chance to know her well. I had no idea she was such an athlete until I discovered what she had done in track and field, and I was really surprised," recalled Doug Harris, filmmaker and producer of *Called Up: The Emmett Ashford Story.*

"Since I was a cheerleader and had a dance class, sometimes we were in the gym at the same time," said former Berkeley High student Phyliss Smith, class of 1978. "I heard about her track achievements years after I graduated. Berkeley High has an event at San Pablo Park on odd years; the event was established by the class of '51, primarily as an 'all class picnic,' and that's where I heard about her career. I didn't know she had achieved such notoriety but was overjoyed that she came from my school. I am happy she is going to have a chapter in this book because she has a sterling reputation and deserves it."

Sherry Sherrard was an Olympic hurdler and Irene's lifelong friend. They met in college in 1957 when they were both students at Chico State; Sherrard was an undergrad, and Obera was getting her teaching credential. They were on the same track team, competed together, and to this day are still good friends. Sherry grew up in California and when asked said she had never had any real problems with people treating her differently because of the color of her skin. She did recall one day, however, many years ago in Texas.

"We were there in 1960 for the Olympic trials and were in a segregated waiting room," Sherrard said. "Irene just sat where she wanted to. She may have been oblivious to the signs, but I was not. I sat in the colored section, while Irene, looking for a seat anywhere, just sat in the white section."

Sherry was in a preliminary heat at the 1964 Olympics in Tokyo, but Irene just missed making the team twice. Sherrard would go on to coach track at Chico State for nine years.

"We all loved 'Reno,'" she recalled. "Irene was a nice person, got along with everybody. They always wanted her to run the relay. Her coach wouldn't let her run the hurdles because he was afraid she might injure herself. Had she started earlier, she would have made the Olympic team. But once she got into the masters, she made up for it."

Obera said she was hell-bent on winning every race she entered. That attitude contributed significantly to her quest for gold after gold. "I simply would not accept defeat," she said in the Masterstrack.com article, "and I'd wait until my time to dominate a race. I'm not signing up for second place." She was relentless in every race she ran.

She set three world indoor records at a meet in March 2014. In the same meet, she participated in the shot put and broke Mary Bowermaster's American record, although, incredibly, it was her first time participating in the event. That same year, she again appeared in *Sports Illustrated*.

"Obera turned 80 last December and celebrated by becoming the oldest woman to break 40 seconds in the 200 meters," the *SI* notice read. "Next week she will run three races at the USA Masters' championships in Boston."

Witnessing Irene in a track meet at Berkeley, one could see she was a fighter and committed to winning every race she participated in. Even in the face of challenges and threats from other runners, Irene was vigilant in protecting her medals position, and extremely focused and committed. In 2019, she made her third appearance in "Faces in the Crowd." *Sports Illustrated* said this: "Obera, 85, earned five gold medals at the WMA indoor championships in Poland."

Although Irene did not make the Olympic team when she was twenty-seven, running the masters seemed to be her calling. She has spent the past forty-seven years as an international track star. In 1996 she was elected into the inaugural class of the USATF Masters' Hall of Fame, and in 2004 she was inducted as a member of the African American Ethnic Sports Hall of Fame.

Obera shared her philosophy in a 2017 video posted on PrimalPlay.com: "To me, I don't think about age as being a handicap. It's just a process. So why not live? Like my father told me, 'Don't ever let race, your sex, gender, or age stand in the way of doing what you want to do.' I believe in the phrase 'If you don't use it, you lose it.' If you are able to find joy in sports, why not continue the pleasure?"

19

Additional Unsung Heroes

THE RENAISSANCE TRAILBLAZER: DON BARKSDALE

An accomplished athlete, radio and television personality, entrepreneur, and philanthropist, Don Barksdale left a significant legacy. The Berkeley, California, native, born in 1923, was cut three years in a row from his high school basketball team because the coach would only allow one Black player on the team. He attended the College of Marin, leading them to two state junior college titles. At UCLA he found time to run a popular record shop, where he honed his entrepreneurial skills. He was the first Black player to be selected to the NCAA All-America basketball team.

Barksdale was also the first Black player in the AAU's American Basketball League, and in 1948 he became the first Black player selected to the U.S. Olympic basketball team. Initially there was racially motivated opposition to Don's inclusion, but after lobbying by his coach and local politicians, he was selected. The team went 8-0 and won a gold medal.

When Don returned home, he hosted *Sepia Review*, a local TV variety show featuring the country's top Black entertainers. "He had his hands in everything," said noted Latin jazz musician Pete Escovedo to filmmaker Doug Harris, producer of the 2016 documentary film *Bounce: The Don Barksdale Story*. "Watching Don's show was like getting a lesson in Black history."

During the summer of 1950, several NBA owners met with Don in an effort to sign him to become the league's first Black player; the new league was basically for white players only. But jumping over to the NBA would have meant he'd have to give up his entertainment career, so he stayed in the AAU where he made the All-America team in each of his four seasons.

In 1951, Barksdale signed a contract with the Baltimore Bullets that made him the fifth-highest-paid player in the league as a twenty-eight-year-old rookie; he averaged 12.6 points and 9.7 rebounds per game. While with the Bullets, in 1953 he became the first African American to appear in an NBA All-Star Game. Shortly afterward, he was traded to the Boston Celtics. He retired from the NBA after the 1955 season, his playing career cut short by ankle injuries. But his work with the Celtics continued off the court. In 1956, he helped Coach Red Auerbach land Bay Area star and future Hall of Famer Bill Russell, who would go on to win eleven titles and become the league's first Black head coach.

After retirement from basketball, Don Barksdale returned to the Bay Area air-waves as a disc jockey and opened up two successful nightclubs. In 1970, Barksdale reinvented himself, returning to work as a scout for the NBA Golden State Warriors, and took on a new direction as a philanthropist. In 1983, he established the Save High School Sports Foundation to provide assistance to keep financially strapped sports programs afloat for student-athletes in Oakland.

"I thought it was a brilliant idea that needed national attention," said author Arif Khatib, "and I was able to introduce it to other parts of the country." He continued, "I remember once Don accompanied me to evaluate a high school player, a family friend. I'll never forget him offering encouragement to that young man after the game."

In 1993, Don Barksdale was stricken with throat cancer and passed away at the age of sixty-nine. In 2022, the College of Marin named their basketball court Don Barksdale Court. Don was inducted into the African American Ethnic Sports Hall of Fame in 2004. His lifelong fight against racism and his contributions to basketball were recognized in 2012 when he was inducted posthumously into the Naismith Memorial Basketball Hall of Fame as a trailblazer and a monumental contributor to the sport.

BEYOND THE FINISH LINE: MAL WHITFIELD

When Mal Whitfield sneaked into the LA Coliseum in the summer of 1932, he saw African American sprinter Eddie Tolan win an Olympic gold medal. The experience ignited a dream for the eight-year-old from Watts. "From that moment on," Whit-field recalled decades later, quoted in his 2015 obituary by the *New York Times*, "I knew I wanted to run in the Olympics."

Mal Whitfield was a champion athlete, a celebrated soldier, and a goodwill ambas-sador for America. He served in the Army Air Force with the famed Tuskegee Airmen and flew twenty-seven combat missions during World War II and the Korean War. He was the Olympic champion in the 800 meters at the 1948 and 1952 Summer

Games and a member of the 1948 gold medal team in the 400-meter relay. "Marvelous Mal" was a five-time Olympic medalist and the first African American to win the James E. Sullivan Award as the most outstanding amateur athlete in the United States. But he experienced racism from hostile crowds on his return from winning a gold medal in 1952.

A patriot who gave a lifetime of service to his country, after his athletic career, Mal pursued a career with the State Department and the U.S. Information Agency. He worked as a goodwill ambassador under five presidents. He lived in Kenya, Uganda, and Egypt; coached in twenty countries; and arranged scholarships for over five thousand African athletes to study in the United States.

His experiences in the Foreign Service involved diplomacy during the Cold War, conducting negotiations with the Chinese and Russians. The respect that he carried within diplomatic circles in Africa afforded him access to the most powerful and influential leaders, which made him one of America's greatest resources on the African political stage.

Whitfield served on a Youth Advisory Committee during the administration of President Eisenhower, represented President Nixon during the 1972 Olympic Games, and met with Presidents Ford, Carter, Reagan, Bush, and Clinton. As chronicled on the Mal Whitfield Foundation's website, President Reagan wrote about Whitfield, "Whether flying combat missions over Korea, winning gold medals at the Olympics, or serving as an ambassador of goodwill, you have given your all. This country is proud of you and grateful to you."

His 2002 book, *Going beyond the Finish Line*, is the inspirational story of an American who dared to dream and turned those dreams into reality. In 2004, at the induction ceremony for the African American Ethnic Sports Hall of Fame, he coined the phrase, "From the auction blocks to the Olympic starting blocks." He was a teammate of gold medalist Alice Coachman, whom he befriended at the 1948 Games in London. In 2008, Whitfield spoke openly about America, race, slavery, and Africa.

In the 2021 documentary film *Because They Believed*, Whitfield spoke on camera about his experience. "Back in those days, America was not really the land of democracy. Black folks were not free, and the world knew that. That's why Blacks went abroad to Europe where they were invited, to pursue their arts and culture. It was a long time before we could sing in opera houses in this country.

"It was not easy being a Black person trying to do your thing," he added. "Even the embassies didn't respect you. There were no Blacks in embassies holding important jobs—they just didn't exist. Everywhere I went in Africa, I never saw more than one Black person in an embassy." But Whitfield left quite an impression on children.

"There are kids from Burundi and Chad who never heard of McDonald's but can quote Mal Whitfield," said his old friend Jim Minnihan in Whitfield's 2015 obituary in the *Los Angeles Times*. "They all look at him as the godfather."

THREE CENTURIES OF BASEBALL: SILAS SIMMONS

Silas Simmons was born in 1895, the same year as Babe Ruth. When he was growing up, it was the era of Ty Cobb, Tris Speaker, Christy Mathewson, Walter "Big Train" Johnson, and "Shoeless" Joe Jackson. It must have been hard for young Silas to get into the ballpark, for these were the days of Jim Crow. And this was long before radio and television brought the stars into your living room.

It was also right before the golden era of the Negro Leagues, with legends like Cool Papa Bell, Josh Gibson, Oscar Charleston, Buck Leonard, and Satchel Paige, men who should have had, but sadly never did have, the chance to make their mark in the big leagues. But even before that time, there were the early Negro Leagues, led by the Pittsburgh-based powerhouse Homestead Grays.

Silas Simmons was raised in the Philadelphia area and began playing semipro ball there around 1910. In 1913, when Silas was eighteen, he joined the Grays. The Negro National League was founded in 1920.

From an early age, Silas was a pitcher, but he also played the outfield. In 1926, when he was thirty, he signed with the New York Lincoln Giants of the Eastern Colored League, who had been the dominant team in African American baseball. That team included John Henry "Pop" Lloyd, generally considered the greatest shortstop in Negro League history.

Simmons recalled that in those early years, in spite of Jim Crow, good players wanted to play against good players, whatever their skin color. But he acknowledged the major leagues' treatment of Black players, both before and after Jackie Robinson. Many players at the time reflected the country's blind racism and claimed that Blacks couldn't play, saying that baseball was "the white man's game."

Ironically, seventy-five years after the color line was broken, the percentage of African American players in pro baseball is now only 7 percent. That is a far cry from the peak of 27 percent in 1975, when Hall of Famers Joe Morgan, Hank Aaron, Reggie Jackson, and Frank Robinson were household names.

In an interview with Dr. Bob Allen for the *African American Sports Magazine* in 2006, Silas Simmons said, "For the Negro League players, you couldn't have a strong league and you couldn't sign contracts because they had no money, and they had no fields to play on." And yet the leagues lasted for decades because of the players and their love of the game.

But Simmons had to make a living, something not always possible on the salary of ballplayers then. He worked at various times as a messenger, in a shoe store, serving his country working in munitions and government-related work during both world wars, and later again in retail, retiring to Florida in 1971.

A plaque was presented to Simmons on his 111th birthday in 2006 on behalf of the Society for American Baseball Research. He died fifteen days later in St. Petersburg, having outlived all five of his children. At the time of his death, Simmons had nine grandchildren, several great-grandchildren, and many great-great-grandchildren. Simmons is also one of the two known professional athletes to have been born in the nineteenth century and died in the twenty-first century.

Some might say Silas Simmons lost the best career years of his life because he could not play in the major leagues. He played the game when it was truly the national pastime. Perhaps one day it will be again.

BORN TO RUN: WILLYE WHITE

"The Olympic Games introduced me to the real world. Before, I thought the whole world consisted of cross burnings and lynchings. After 1956 I found there were two worlds, Mississippi and the rest of the world. The Olympics taught me not to judge a person by the color of their skin, but by the contents of their hearts," said Willye White in an interview with Dr. Bob Allen in the 2006 issue of the *African American Sports Magazine*.

Willye White was born in 1939 in Money, Mississippi. Within days, her parents abandoned her. Raised by her maternal grandparents, she spent summers working in the cotton fields. Her grandfather instilled in her lessons that stayed with her.

"He taught me the value of work," White said in the 2006 interview. "And that life offers choices. He said that I could get pregnant and spend the rest of my life in the fields, or I could get an education and get out. Athletics were my freedom from ignorance and segregation."

Just sixteen and a speedy high school sophomore, she found a way out of the Mississippi delta. She qualified for the 1956 Olympic Games and traveled to Melbourne, where she narrowly missed a gold medal in the long jump, taking a silver medal home.

It was in Australia that White said she realized the world was different. She returned home and enrolled at Tennessee State University, where, under the tutelage of legendary coach Ed Temple, she was a member of the famed Tigerbelles track team.

She qualified in the long jump for the Rome 1960 Olympics, where TSU teammate Wilma Rudolph won three gold medals. At the 1964 Games in Tokyo, White won a silver medal in the 4×100-meter relay. She participated in the long jump in both the 1968 and 1972 Games.

White competed in more than 150 nations as a member of international track teams. She was the first American woman to participate in five Olympic Games, following that with a long career as a nurse, civil servant, and coach. She moved to Chicago in 1960 and was kept out of nursing school by a racial quota, but she eventually got her license in 1963. In 1965, she became a public health administrator for the city and in 1976 graduated with a BA in public health from Chicago State. She remained active in sports, coaching track athletes.

A year later, she started a foundation to develop self-esteem and help young people become productive citizens through athletics; she also taught children living in the nation's largest housing project.

White was the first American to win the world's highest sportsmanship award, the UNESCO Fair Play Trophy. She is a member of eleven sports halls of fame, including the African American Ethnic Sports Hall of Fame. Respected and loved by other athletes and with an ebullient personality, at major meets and Olympic trials her suite was the place to be.

She was chosen by *Sports Illustrated* in 1999 as one of the one hundred greatest female athletes of the century, and by *Ebony* in 2002 as one of the ten greatest Black female athletes. Willye White died in 2007 at age sixty-seven. She left a legacy of pride, perseverance, and public service.

White's motto was, "If it is to be, it is up to me, for I believe in me. It took me 57 years to find the job of my life," she said in Michael Davis's 1992 book, *Black American Women in Olympic Track and Field*. "This is my ministry. When you jump in competition, it is measured by inches. I won the gold medal in life by a mile."

From her 2007 *New York Times* obituary, "In 1993, she told *Runner's World*: 'Athletics was my flight to freedom: freedom from prejudice, freedom from illiteracy, freedom from bias. It was my acceptance in the world.'"

THE GODFATHER OF JUDO: YOSHIHIRO UCHIDA

Yoshihiro Uchida, born in California's Imperial Valley in 1920 to Japanese immigrant farm laborers, started his collegiate career at Fullerton Junior College, just outside of Los Angeles, in 1938. Uchida hoped to work in the petroleum industry. That was until a professor told him that he was wasting his time. In 2007, writer Urla Hill put together the *Speed City Era: The Coaches* exhibition at San Jose State University and included Uchida, whom she interviewed at the time. He recalled the professor asking him, "Why are you majoring in chemistry? You are not going to get a job. No company will hire Japanese."

He was encouraged to take part in the sporting activities on campus and in fall 1941 took over the judo program. Following the bombing of Pearl Harbor on December 7, Uchida's family was among the 127,000 Japanese on the mainland sent to internment camps. While his parents were sent to a camp in Poston, Arizona, Uchida was drafted into the army, where he served as a medic in the Midwest. Just like Black Americans, Japanese Americans were forced to serve in segregated units. Although the Japanese recruits trained with whites, they were not sent out on the same types of missions.

"We did everything but military work," Uchida said in the San Jose State interview.

Upon the war's end, Uchida's parents and brothers returned to Japan. He and his sister remained in the United States, and he took over the campus judo program at San Jose State University in 1946. He quickly found out that he was not welcomed by the returning soldiers.

One afternoon a 6'4" soldier, a football player, posed a question to Uchida, who recalled him asking, "What can a Jap teach me? We used to use people like you for bayonet practice."

"I told him, 'I don't know,'" he told Hill. "Why don't you come over here and find out?" said Uchida, who stands 5'4". The student picked Uchida up, dangled him in front of the other students, and laughed. Uchida used his leverage, flipped the student, and elbowed him in the chest; the student could barely breathe. "After that, I didn't have any more problems," Uchida said.

Off campus, Uchida encountered hostility in the community. The public had not forgotten the attack on Pearl Harbor. Upon their return from the camps, the Japanese found that their housing and other property had been sold or destroyed. Those who had hopes of resettling throughout California were subject to hate crimes.

In 1962, Uchida organized the first collegiate nationals. Judo was established as an Olympic sport, and in 1964, he coached the first U.S. Olympic team. Through Uchida's guidance, judo changed from a method of self-defense to a full-fledged intercollegiate sport. He was inducted into the San Jose Sports Hall of Fame in 1996. In 1997, the judo dojo on campus was renamed Yoshihiro Uchida Hall. Ironically, Uchida's family was processed in this building prior to being sent to an internment camp during World War II. In 2006, Yoshiro Uchida was inducted into the African American Ethnic Sports Hall of Fame.

As of 2012, his Spartan judo teams have won forty-five of the fifty-one National Collegiate Judo Championships. Several years ago, Uchida thought about retiring and approached the administration at San Jose State. "I was told that if I retired, there would be no more judo," said Uchida in the exhibit.

Mike Swain, a four-time Olympian who runs the San Jose State judo club with Uchida, was asked about the coach on the occasion of Uchida's one hundredth birthday party in April 2020. "He has been through a lot," Swain said. "He's a fighter who doesn't give up."

Yoshihiro Uchida has ensured that San Jose State's judo program will remain a part of his legacy.

PRINCE OF THE PELOTON: MARSHALL "MAJOR" TAYLOR

Around the turn of the nineteenth century, bicycle racing was a popular sport, especially in Europe, where huge crowds would show up to watch young men sprint on bikes that weighed twice as much as the high-tech carbon fiber road bikes of today.

In 1895, out of the Midwest came a young African American man, an athletic rider who could do amazing things on a bike, from circus tricks to riding faster than the wind. He made quick work of his opponents and the cycling records.

But respect was nowhere to be found in his homeland, a young country only thirty years removed from a civil war that was fought to free his people, but succeeded in name only. The Black codes and the Jim Crow laws made sure of that.

Born on a farm in rural Indiana in 1878, his parents had migrated from Kentucky; his grandparents and parents had been slaves. His father was a Civil War veteran, his mother a housekeeper who raised eight children.

The 1890s were a time when Jim Crow laws were at their height; Taylor was excluded from bicycle clubs, threatened with death, forced to crash into fences by his rivals, and barred from the YMCA where other racers trained. Still he persisted.

He traveled to Europe where he found success, fortune, and fame, and most importantly respect. There Marshall flew up the ranks. In France, where he was very popular, they nicknamed him "*Le Negre Volant*," the Black Cyclone.

Taylor dominated racing in the United States, Europe, and Australia between 1901 and 1904, beating the world's greatest racers. Yet he could not enjoy his success during or after the glory years on the velodromes. He was a man who overcame tremendous obstacles, who was committed to his art, the thing we all learn to do as kids—riding a bike.

As his successes mounted, Marshall had to fend off racial insults and attacks from fellow cyclists and cycling fans. While he'd been the object of much respect and attention in France and Europe, in the American South, Taylor was barred from racing.

By 1910, Taylor was still breaking records, but discrimination and tactics aimed at stopping him from excelling in America limited his opportunities. By the 1920s, he had lost everything to bad investments, one of which was the self-publishing of his 1928 autobiography, *The Fastest Bicycle Rider in the World*. In the foreword, he wrote,

"I am writing my memoirs to solicit simple justice, equal rights and a square deal for the posterity of my downtrodden but brave people, not only in athletic games and sports, but in every honorable game of human endeavor."

Marshall Taylor passed away in 1932, just fifty-four. On his headstone is engraved the following:

World's champion bicycle racer who came up the hard way
An honest, courageous, and God-fearing, clean living gentlemanly athlete,
He always gave out his best, gone but not forgotten.

Taylor was a blindingly fast cyclist when the sport was the most popular in America and Europe, thrilling fans on three continents. He was a Black man in America when segregation ruled the nation, and he was a man of faith who believed in forgiveness.

"Life is too short for a man to hold bitterness in his heart," said Marshall Taylor in his autobiography.

"PUT IN THE BATBOY!": JOE RELIFORD

On a hot summer night in July 1952 in Statesboro, Georgia, a twelve-year-old batboy made history. They say that every day you go to the ballpark you see something you've never seen before. On a muggy night in Georgia, five thousand fans witnessed the youngest player to ever play in a pro baseball game.

Joe Louis Reliford was born in 1939 in the small town of Fitzgerald, in South Georgia, the ninth of ten children in a family of sharecroppers. A talented athlete, Joe played sandlot baseball and followed both of the town's pro teams, the Fitzgerald Lucky Stars of the Negro Leagues and the all-white Class D Pioneers, who at the time played in the Georgia State League.

Due to segregation laws, he had to watch the games from a nearby tree. When he was ten, he asked team manager Ace Adams if he could be the batboy. Soon Joe was earning a salary of $24 per week and traveling to road games. Adams assured Joe's mother that he would be safe. The team's players embraced the batboy, teaching him skills after practice.

On July 19, 1952, the Pioneers traveled to Statesboro, Georgia. The night before, the teams had played a close game in Fitzgerald featuring two controversial calls by the home plate umpire, both of which went against the home team. The umpire's tires were slashed and his gas tank filled with sand. Consequently, the Pioneers were fined $200 and placed on probation.

At the game the next night, Statesboro was leading 13–0 in the eighth inning; the fans got restless and chanted, "Put in the batboy!" The Pioneers' road manager,

Charlie Ridgeway, who had a fondness for the kid, spoke to the ump. When he came back to the dugout, he told Reliford to grab a bat. With the game out of reach, Ridgeway decided to give the rowdy fans what they wanted. With the approval of the umpire, Reliford strode to the plate.

On the first pitch, the twelve-year-old pulled a sharp grounder to the third baseman, whose throw barely beat the fleet Reliford. In the bottom of the inning, Ridgeway sent Reliford out to right field. The leadoff hitter hammered a pitch into the gap and decided to test the youngster's arm. Reliford retrieved the ball and fired to the cutoff man, who nailed the runner at third.

The next batter hit a long fly to right field. At the fence, Reliford made a leaping catch, robbing him of an extra-base hit. After the game, the fans streamed onto the field to congratulate the twelve-year-old and stuff money in his pockets. The following day, the league fired the umpire and suspended Ridgeway for five days. The league said that the two had made a travesty of the game by allowing an ineligible player to play.

Reliford went on to letter in four sports in high school and earned a football scholarship to Florida A&M, but his athletic career was cut short by a knee injury. After graduation, Reliford went on to become an electrician and moved to the nearby town of Douglas, where he was later appointed deputy sheriff, a post he held until retiring in 1998. Today, Joe Reliford lives in Douglas and spends much of his time with his sixteen grandchildren. And he is still the youngest player to appear in a pro game.

A LIFE IN THE SWEET SCIENCE: THELL TORRENCE

He was an up-and-coming middleweight contender in 1965 who came within one punch of a shot at the crown. But he found his calling teaching and inspiring others. It is not just his many accomplishments that separate Thell Torrence; it is his commitment to the sport, to the pursuit of excellence and discipline in and out of the ring, and to the dozens of young men whose lives he has touched, molding them into productive men whose successes mirror the guidance he gave them.

Growing up in Camden, Arkansas, Torrence starred on the hardwood and the gridiron. He learned how to box from a local trainer, joined the navy, and in 1959 won the navy light middleweight title and captured the California Golden Gloves middleweight title.

While working out in Los Angeles, Torrence was approached by legendary trainer Eddie Futch, who trained Joe Frazier, Ken Norton, Larry Holmes, and Trevor Berbick, all of whom defeated Muhammad Ali. Futch became his manager; their relationship would last more than four decades. Thell Torrence's career consisted of only fourteen fights. But he has no regrets. Looking back, he wouldn't trade his years with Eddie Futch for a dozen championship belts. But if he could go back in time, he would erase the final ten seconds of one fight.

Torrence and Irish Denny Moyer met at the Olympic Auditorium in LA on October 14, 1965. Moyer was a middleweight who owned victories over Emile Griffith and Sugar Ray Robinson. Entering the final round, Thell was ahead on the scorecards. Then, with only ten seconds remaining, he was knocked down by one punch. Moyer skirted defeat, salvaging a draw. Torrence had one more fight and then called it quits. "I can see that punch coming to this very day," he said in a 2016 interview with Arne Lang for the publication *The Sweet Science*.

After retiring in 1968, Torrence purchased the Hoover Street Gym in LA where he trained some of the world's top boxers, among them world champions Riddick Bowe and Ken Norton. He eventually settled in Las Vegas. "There are countless ways to train a fighter," said Thell in *Sweet Science*, "and to be successful, you must have one who has the will, ability and determination."

"When I became a licensed promoter, the first person I was introduced to by Dick Sadler was Thell Torrence," said Arif Khatib. "A good trainer can turn a mediocre fighter into a champion. A fighter looks to the trainer for guidance and reassurance. Dick wanted me involved with Thell for many reasons. Thell provided me with the incentive I needed to move my company forward. Fighters I spoke with said Torrence spends a lot of time with his fighters in his gym. Since he was a fighter himself, his belief in codifying his approach to training is what helped them become a better fighter."

"I first went to him in 1993, and Thell was like a father to me. I'm now a trainer, and I use what I learned from him even today." From the *Sweet Science* interview, these are the words of Montell "Ice" Griffin, who rose to prominence when he defeated middleweight champ James Toney twice, in 1995 and 1996.

"Working by his side I have seen a man who has given his heart and soul to boxers," said his longtime manager Shelley Williams when interviewed. "And under his tutelage they fulfilled their dreams of becoming World Champions."

THE CHECKERED FLAG: WILLY T. RIBBS

Willy T. Ribbs isn't a household name outside of the world of race cars, but he should be. During the 1980s, he was one of the fastest drivers around any racetrack, oval, road course, or circuit. He had world-class talent, skill, drive, and determination, enough to become an internationally famous racer—if it weren't for the color of his skin.

Willy T. Ribbs was born in San Jose, California, in 1955. His father raced as a hobby, and from an early age, Willy grew up with cars and motorcycles. His dad was a no-nonsense man who allowed his children to make their own mistakes, but he expected them to be accountable and carry their own weight. For Willy T. Ribbs and countless others of his generation, Muhammad Ali was the top role model. Ali reminded him of the toughness he was raised with. Another was Jim Brown.

Ribbs is an outspoken Black man who received criticism for his forthrightness during his career, sometimes from other African Americans in auto racing. Ribbs went to England when he was twenty-one, found immediate success, and was on the fast track to becoming an elite international race car driver.

"The drivers over there, they didn't look at me other than that I was an American," said Ribbs in a 2008 interview with Dr. Bob Allen in the *African American Sports Magazine*. "You were like everyone else—you were a driver. That's how they dealt with me; as a driver, not a Black driver."

In 1986, he became the first Black driver to test a Formula One car, twenty-one years before current superstar Lewis Hamilton, a British driver who has won six titles driving for Mercedes. That same year, Ribbs competed twice in the NASCAR Cup series.

In 1991, he became the first African American to qualify for the Indianapolis 500, and he qualified again in 1993. But by 1994 it was clear that corporate sponsors were not willing to back an African American sports car driver. However, entertainer Bill Cosby stepped up and offered to finance him. Willy accepted his offer, and Cosby become his sponsor.

Ribbs has spoken negatively about his experience in NASCAR. In May 2006, a newspaper column quoted Ribbs referring to NASCAR as "Neckcar." In 2020, Bubba Wallace, an up-and-coming Black NASCAR driver, put the words "Black Lives Matter" on the side of his competition car and called on the sport to get rid of Confederate flags at races. And they did.

"Auto racing is an elitist sport," Willy said in the 2008 interview. "Most of the people come from wealthy backgrounds. So the young kids that get into it are raised to think that they are better based on their privileged background. And my attitude was, 'Hey, I come from just as big a background as you.'"

In 2006, Ribbs was inducted into the African American Ethnic Sports Hall of Fame. In 2020, the film *Uppity: The Willy T. Ribbs Story*, an in-depth profile of his life and career, was released on Netflix. The film received outstanding reviews and at one point occupied the number one slot on Netflix movies.

The film captures it all, and in doing so doesn't overplay the racial narratives. It's history told by Ribbs himself. He's a very down-to-earth storyteller, and a who's who of the racing world has his back. It's an important biography, one about our past and the power of positive thought, one that today's young people would benefit from watching.

THE SHOT HEARD AROUND THE WORLD: JOE GAETJENS

Born in Port-au-Prince, Haiti, in 1924, Joe Gaetjens developed a love for soccer at an early age. Of mixed African and European heritage, his was a wealthy family by Haitian standards. He grew up playing pickup soccer without coaches or referees, enabling him to develop the confidence that served him well later in his career. At fourteen, he became the youngest member of one of the island's top teams, the Haitian Stars. By age twenty, he had led them to two championships.

In 1947, his parents sent him to Columbia University to study accounting. He became a dishwasher at a local restaurant in New York City, where he met people connected to the local soccer leagues, and he joined Brookhattan Galicia of the American Soccer League. By season's end, Joe had been so impressive that he was selected to the U.S. national team heading to Brazil for the 1950 World Cup.

In the aftermath of World War II, Germany and Japan were not allowed to qualify. Other countries refused to participate in the qualifying tournament or simply dropped out, citing costs. Turkey, India, Scotland, and France withdrew after qualifying. Most of the teams that came to Rio de Janeiro had professional players. Team USA was a different story.

England prided itself as the founder of the modern game, and they were confident; their squad entered the tournament as the favorites. Team USA entered as a 500–1 long shot. England started off with a win over Chile. That same day, the USA lost to Spain, 3–1.

When the teams met, the game went as expected, as the English attacked from the beginning. But they could not score, as the U.S. men played stout defense. The magic moment came at thirty-eight minutes. Gaetjens, with a diving header, sent the ball in the opposite direction into the net, barely eluding the goalie to register the only goal of the game. Jubilant fans that made up the pro-USA crowd carried him on their shoulders after the stunning 1–0 victory.

After the World Cup, Gaetjens signed with Racing Club de Paris, but he found soccer in France much different than what he had experienced in both Haiti and the United States. It was more disciplined and less fun. By 1952, he was injured and disaffected. For Gaetjens, it was time to come home.

Though Gaetjens himself was not political, some family members actively opposed "Papa Doc" Duvalier, the brutal authoritarian dictator. Two of his brothers had emigrated to neighboring Dominican Republic as part of an effort to plot a revolution.

Duvalier had no tolerance for political opposition. When he could not go after opponents, he targeted their family members. Consequently, Joe Gaetjens was taken away by the dreaded Tonton Macoute secret police in July 1964 and brought to the notorious Fort Dimanche prison. Although his body was never found, Gaetjens is presumed to have died two days later.

"I used to pray every night for my father to come back," his son Lesly said in his book about his father titled *The Shot Heard Around the World*. "I always had that emptiness, and I always had that feeling of, 'OK, maybe he's going to show up.'"

Joe Gaetjens was unknown at the time of his greatest sporting feat. But he will go down forever as the man who made the shot heard around the world.

PIONEER OF THE DIAMOND, ACE OF THE ICE: MANNY MCINTYRE

In Canada in the 1940s, there was a gifted athlete so talented that he could have played both professional baseball and hockey at the highest level. But he was of mixed race, and the doors to those elite rooms were closed. Yet his character and perseverance were such that his achievements were not diminished by those obstacles.

In 1946, he became the first Black Canadian to play professional baseball, and between 1941 and 1949 he was a member of the famous "Colored Line" of Canadian hockey with brothers Herb and Ossie Carnegie, also known as the "Black Aces." He dealt with discrimination on and off the field and the ice and emerged with grace, kindness, and a positive attitude. His name was Manny McIntyre.

Born in New Brunswick in 1918, his ancestors were of Irish and African descent. In school he was an accomplished athlete and moved to senior hockey when he was eighteen, playing all over eastern Canada. He played one season in France, where Black artists and athletes found acceptance. In baseball, he played with the New York Cubans of the American Negro League.

Manny was a pioneer, making a living playing baseball in summer and hockey in winter. But he lived in a time and place that did not provide athletes of color the same opportunities as others. In 1950, a waitress in New Brunswick refused to serve the team if Manny was included; so they all left without eating.

Manny was good enough to play in the NHL, and if not baseball's big leagues, certainly in the minors, yet he was excluded from both. In spite of that, he loved life and lived it to the fullest. His charismatic personality drew people to him.

In 1946, five Black American players drawn from the Negro Leagues, led by Jackie Robinson, entered organized baseball. Manny McIntyre was the only Canadian who did, signing a contract with the Sherbrooke Canadians.

Although hitting .310, a hockey injury to his throwing arm ended his career early. But it was also the isolation by his teammates, white Americans who were supportive on the diamond but not off the field. In spite of his potential to play pro baseball, scouts were no longer interested, and the door was closed.

Manny is best known as a member of Canadian hockey's famous "Colored Line" with Herb and Ossie Carnegie. From 1944 to 1949, the trio played with the Sherbrooke Saints of the Quebec Senior Hockey League and regularly led the league in scoring. Herb was a playmaker at center, Ossie a wing with a wicked shot, and Manny was on the left wing, controlling the corners and delivering bone-crushing forechecks.

The "Colored Line" was highly respected, although there were racial epithets thrown at them. Hall of Famer Jean Béliveau is quoted in a biographical virtual presentation about McIntyre by Canadian writer John Lutz titled "Manny McIntyre: Elite Athlete & Sports Pioneer": "I believe that the whole line could have and should have played in the NHL," he said.

Manny returned to the Maritimes, finishing his career in Quebec and becoming a role model. "I am not bitter about not making the NHL," he said in Lutz's presentation. "I know that I was good enough, and that is good enough for me."

Manny McIntyre was a special athlete, a trailblazer who hopefully will someday receive the proper recognition and be acknowledged for his contributions.

MENTOR OF THE RING AND PITCH: JULIUS MENENDEZ

Julius Menendez was nineteen when he joined the navy shortly after the bombing of Pearl Harbor. Unlike the African American and Japanese American recruits during that period, Hispanic Americans did not serve in segregated ranks and had limited roles. So Menendez entered with aspirations of becoming a naval pilot.

Following the death of one of his peers, however, he and other young pilots in the unit received transfers. Menendez, who had been boxing since his early teens, opted for the boxing unit in Athens, Georgia. It was there that he encountered San Jose State boxing coach DeWitt Portal. With a bit of encouragement following the war, Menendez joined Portal on San Jose's campus in 1946.

Like fellow San Jose State alumnus Dr. Harry Edwards, who made a name for himself along with John Carlos and Tommie Smith in the sports world, Menendez hailed from East St. Louis, Illinois. Though Menendez and Edwards grew up a decade apart, the face of their hometown throughout those years was the same: crime, drugs, and a lack of educational opportunities limited the growth of the city's immigrant and minority populations.

"He told me that Portal took a lot of flak for bringing a person to campus who didn't speak English that well," said his son Jack in the San Jose State 2007 exhibit, *Speed City Era: The Coaches*. "And people didn't like the fact that he was a professional boxer. But I think it had more to do with his English. The story I got was he was so worried about what people thought that he learned to speak English with no accent." As a result, Menendez majored in English and graduated magnum cum laude.

He went on to coach the boxing team, leading the Spartans to three consecutive NCAA titles from 1958 to 1960. In 1960, he coached the U.S. Olympic boxing team to five gold medals and one silver. That team featured a brash young Kentucky light heavyweight named Cassius Clay—now better known as Muhammad Ali.

Menendez stopped coaching boxing in 1960. But he had started coaching soccer starting in 1954 at San Jose State. After the 1960 Olympics, he continued coaching the men's soccer team, which he revived upon his return to campus. He would go on to coach thirty-six seasons, up to 1990.

But winning championships and winning gold medals in the Olympics was not enough to make a difference in buying a house where he wanted. Doors were shut because he was Hispanic. A group of sportswriters began making phone calls, and eventually the family was able to purchase the house of their choice.

Menendez's soccer coaching career continued to flourish, and he is credited with popularizing soccer in the city of San Jose. He built an international reputation by serving as a committee consultant, including the U.S. Olympic Committee and the NCAA. He also coached boxing for the U.S. military boxing team and put on boxing clinics throughout the world.

Julius Menendez was a big part of the athletic history of San Jose and the only American to coach U.S. national teams in two sports. Menendez was inducted into the African American Ethnic Sports Hall of Fame in 2006. He passed away two days before his ninety-first birthday in 2013.

"My dad was famous; everybody knew him," his son Jack wrote in the San Jose State exhibit.

A WINNER NEVER QUITS: EDDIE HART

When Eddie Hart was growing up in Martinez, California, he was a young runner with a dream. His father, who had survived the Port Chicago blast where 320 died, two-thirds of whom were African American sailors, had impressed upon his son the importance of being the best at whatever he chose to do.

In 1970, Eddie Hart won the NCAA championships in the 100-meter run as a University of California student, and at the Olympic trials in 1972 he equaled the world record, running the 100 meters in 9.9 seconds. He was favored to win the race at the Olympic Games and was soon off to Munich.

But a tragedy occurred; on the day of his quarterfinal heat, a scheduling snafu resulted in his disqualification when he arrived seconds after the race started. His childhood dream, to become the world's fastest human, was shattered.

In a recent interview with the authors, Eddie shared some of his experiences. "Stan Wright, our coach, told us we had time to rest before the quarterfinals. But Stan had the wrong schedule. The ABC TV crew piled us into their van, and we sped to the stadium. Halfway through the tunnel, I heard a starting gun go off. It was the gun for my race. It hurt," Hart said, recalling crying in the shower, "but I took it as an opportunity."

Many faulted Stan Wright, but he had been given the wrong schedule by officials. Hart never cast blame on Wright.

"I never, ever, for a second, had any ill feelings towards him," said Hart.

After the tragic murder of eleven Israeli athletes halted the Games, there was still a relay race to run. With Eddie running anchor, the USA won the gold medal.

Eddie was asked if what happened in Munich fifty years ago still bothers him.

"Yes, but not in the way that most people think," said Hart. "And when I think back on that experience, the most difficult part for me wasn't about me. What hurt the most was how it affected the people that were in my corner. I also see it as a defining moment in my life. To this day, I feel as good about the way I handled it as I did when it happened."

Hart became a teacher and coach at the college level. His Eddie Hart All in One Foundation promotes youth education and physical health through clinics, workshops, and other programs. We asked Eddie about the activities of the foundation.

"We run a program for the Pittsburg School District, doing field trips and providing equipment to youth whose families can't afford it," he said. "Eighty percent of the students are on some sort of government program. So we help them get into college, contacting coaches on their behalf, writing letters when needed." The foundation's Olympian Track Education Clinic provides Olympians to work with these aspiring track and field athletes.

Eddie spoke to his experience with racism growing up.

"As little kids, we were trick-or-treating, and at this one house this guy opens the door and says to his wife, 'I'm not giving candy to these kids.' He had a gun in his hand. I told my brother, we ain't gettin' any candy here."

He continued, "I grew up in a diverse community, and there was a Pop Warner team that was undefeated, but some teams wouldn't play them because they had Black athletes."

"Eddie Hart is a special individual, soft-spoken and sincere, filled with forgiveness. He remains an integral part of Olympic lore," said Dave Newhouse, coauthor with Eddie Hart of *Disqualified: Eddie Hart, Munich 1972, and the Voices of the Most Tragic Olympics.*

WITH PEN AND PAPER, HE MADE HIS MARK: SAM LACY

We would be remiss if we did not include a shout-out to the fourth estate, in this case, two journalists who courageously covered the social and political aspects of sports as well as athletes' accomplishments on the field. Their efforts changed hearts and minds, using the power of the written and spoken word to bring attention to minority athletes and bring them recognition and inclusion into the highest ranks of their chosen sport.

For Sam Lacy, his commitment to the story was only equaled by his drive to get to the truth. He dealt with the ugly specter of racism for most of his life, and he lived long enough not only to see Babe Ruth and Barry Bonds play, but to see the civil rights movement take shape. He witnessed the dawn of free agency and the success of Black managers and coaches in the pro ranks.

Lacy was raised in the nation's capital during the Jim Crow era; it was a southern city with a predominantly Black populace. He was an energetic boy who grew up fetching balls for white ballplayers at a long-gone stadium where, in its heyday, one could hear the sounds of segregation and the demons of discrimination shouting from the stands. As a gifted young athlete, he wanted to follow his dream, but in the America of the 1920s, that was not possible.

So he went to college, developed his writing skills, and through hard work became a brilliant journalist. He covered the biggest stories and was a tireless advocate for athletes of color. Lacy was the first to crusade against the bigoted inequity of baseball's color line. Before Jackie Robinson entered the big leagues, Sam Lacy engineered a one-man campaign to integrate Major League Baseball.

In 1940, he joined the *Chicago Defender*, a Black newspaper founded in 1905, advocating for integration and progressive causes against anti-Semitism. While at the *Defender*, Lacy started a letter-writing campaign to Major League Baseball owners.

"A man whose skin is white or red or yellow has been acceptable. But a man whose character may be of the highest and whose ability may be Ruthian has been barred completely from the sport because he is colored," Lacy wrote in a 1945 column for the *Baltimore Afro American*.

Lacy was barred from press boxes for decades because of his color. But his eloquence was unmatched. In 1997, Lacy, ninety-three, was awarded the Spink Award for outstanding baseball writing from the Baseball Writers' Association, which carries induction to the Baseball Hall of Fame. He spoke that day:

"In 1966, when Ted Williams was inducted," Lacy said, "he said he hoped that someday players in the Negro Leagues would be recognized. My presence here today should, I hope, impress upon the public that the Negro press has a role that should be recognized and honored."

In 2003, Sam Lacy was honored in Philadelphia by the African American Ethnic Sports Hall of Fame. Although he was not inducted, he received a special award at the ceremony.

Mr. Lacy continued writing until he died in 2003 at the age of ninety-nine. He wrote his last column from the hospital. On October 30, 2019, the Washington Nationals, heir to the long-departed Senators, won their first World Series title since Walter Johnson, the "Big Train," led them to a championship in 1924, the year Sam Lacy turned twenty-one. He would have been proud.

HE TOLD IT LIKE IT WAS: "BIG SAM" SKINNER

Broadcaster and journalist Sam Skinner came of age in the 1960s and covered several historic stories, from the 1968 Olympic bravery of Tommie Smith and John Carlos to the horror of the 1972 Munich Olympics. He was the first to integrate the press box, which for decades had been the domain of the good old boys' club.

Skinner was born in Texas, grew up in San Francisco, and remained in the Bay Area his entire adult life, where he carved out a career in radio and broadcast sports journalism. He was a big, joyful man who knew everyone, making friends along the way with names like Ali, Madden, Montana, and Abdul-Jabbar. During a period when the popularity and profits of sports soared, his was a reassuring and knowledgeable voice who brought those contests to life on the radio.

Sam was often the first Black person in stadium and arena press boxes. For three decades, his distinctive voice, affable nature, and outgoing personality welcomed young reporters to those sanctuaries. He was one of the best, a man who did his homework and brought knowledge and style to the job.

Former all-star pitcher and world champion Dave Stewart, an Oakland native, remembered listening to Skinner's radio broadcasts as a child and having a special bond with Skinner when he was a player in Oakland. "He was one guy you'd tell something to you probably wouldn't tell the other writers," Stewart said in a 1996 piece about Skinner by Rob Gloster for AP News.

After graduating from the University of San Francisco, he took a job as a copy boy at the *San Francisco Examiner* and eventually became a sportswriter there. He went on to work at the *California Voice*, the oldest Black newspaper in California. As a radio reporter for KDIA AM 1310, his voice reached thousands of listeners in Northern California.

The presence of five major sports teams in the area helped promote interest on the air, and Big Sam was a fixture for years, known for the tag line he'd deliver at the end of every radio show: "And if you can't be a good sport, don't bother to play the game."

Skinner was a go-between for white sportswriters and the Black athletes they covered and earned a reputation for getting athletes to talk to him when they wouldn't talk to any other reporter. This proved indispensable at the 1968 Olympics in Mexico City when San Jose State track stars John Carlos and Tommie Smith gave Black power salutes while accepting medals. Smith and Carlos trusted Sam to report the truth about their courageous action.

The impact Sam Skinner had on Black journalists' ability to gain access to post-game interviews was important. "At that time, press credentials were extremely difficult to obtain as an African American," said Arif Khatib. "Sam was responsible for getting me an NBA credential for Warrior games, and he insisted that I sit with him on the floor, courtside. He helped me create a relationship with the team that exists today."

The Golden State Warriors named the media lounge and workroom in the new Oakland Arena after him and established a Sam Skinner Good Guy Award that is presented annually to a local sports journalist. The Good Guy award is fitting, because Big Sam Skinner was, with all of his prodigious talents, above all else, a good guy.

Bibliography

Abeel, Daphne. "Edward Gourdin, Brief Life of a Breaker of Barriers." *Harvard Magazine*, 1 December 1997.

Abrahamson, Alan. "Shame on the Games." *Los Angeles Times*, 5 January 2001.

Ackmann, Martha. *Curveball: The Remarkable Story of Toni Stone, the First Woman to Play Professional Baseball in the Negro League*. Chicago: Chicago Review Press, 2010.

Adrian, Jad. "Chi Cheng the Greatest Asian Sprinter of All Time." Adrian Sprints, 2011, http://www.adriansprints.com/2011/08/chi-cheng-greatest-asian-sprinter-of.html (accessed 3 August 2021).

"Alice Coachman." Biography, 2014, https://www.biography.com/athlete/alice-coachman (accessed 29 July 2020).

Allen, Bob. "Put in the Batboy." *African American Sports Magazine*, 2007.

Allen, Bob. "Running the Good Race." *African American Sports Magazine*, 2008.

Allen, Bob. "The Last Survivor." *African American Sports Magazine*, 2006.

Allen, Bob. "The Olympian and the Gold Within." *African American Sports Magazine*, 2007.

Alonso Hernandez, Martha. "At 104, Millito Navarro Is America's Outstanding Oldest Male Worker." Latina Lista, 6 August 2010.

Associated Press. "Foster, First Black Student at University of Alabama, Dies." 2 March 2022.

Barra, Allen. "How Curt Flood Changed Baseball and Killed His Career in the Process." *The Atlantic*, 12 July 2011, https://www.theatlantic.com/entertainment/archive/2011/07/how-curt-flood-changed-baseball-and-killed-his-career-in-the-process/241783 (accessed 12 December 2020).

BBWAA Career Excellence (Spinks) Award. Baseball Hall of Fame 1997, https://baseballhall.org/discover-more/awards/spink/sam-lacy (accessed 21 March 2022).

Brijnath, Rohit. "50 Years Ago World's Fastest Woman Was an Asian." *Straits Times*, 5 July 2020, https://www.straitstimes.com/sport/50-years-ago-worlds-fastest-woman-was-an-asian (accessed 5 July 2021).

Carr, Susan, and Doug Harris. "Justin Carr Speaks about His Grandfather." Video tribute to Justin Carr, 2013, www.justincarrwantsworldpeace.org (accessed 7 October 2020).

Chi Cheng. "Chi Cheng, Iron Girl Champion." *Taiwan Review*, 1970, https://taiwantoday.tw/news.php?unit=29,45&post=36808 (accessed 1 April 2022).

Choi, Minju. "Anti-Asian Hate Is Still on the Rise. Ending It Has to Start in the Classroom." *SF Chronicle*, 6 March 2022.

Coachman, Alice. "Gold Medal Moments." Video produced by Team USA, part of the USA Olympic Committee, 2008, www.youtube.com/watch?v=n8GdDQocz2 (accessed 17 May 2021).

Coachman, Alice. "Obituary." *Telegraph*, 15 July 2014, https://www.telegraph.co.uk/news/obituaries/10968896/Alice-Coachman-obituary.html.

College of San Mateo Centennial. "Archie Williams (CSM Class of 1935)." 2022. www.collegeofsanmateo.edu (accessed 3 February 2022).

Constable, George. *The Olympic Century: XI, XII, & XIII Olympiads*. Los Angeles: World Sport Research & Publications, 1996.

Davis, Merlene. "Female Baseball Player Got the Ball Rolling." *Lexington Herald-Leader*, 28 November 1996.

Davis, Michael D. *Black American Women in Olympic Track and Field*. Jefferson, NC: McFarland, 1992.

Dean, Amy, "Edward Gourdin: Olympic Silver Medalist, but a Man of Firsts." *BU Bridge*, 15 February 2002.

Denney, Bob. "Remembering Pete Brown—The Man Who Deflected Hate and Won Many Hearts." *PGA Championship News*, https://www.pgachampionship.com/news-media/remembering-pete-brown-the-man-who-deflected-hate-and-won-many-hearts (accessed 9 February 2022).

Dickey, Glenn. "Hitler's Games: A High Time for Gold Medalist." *San Francisco Chronicle*, 12 June 1984.

Edwards, Bob. "Mamie 'Peanut' Johnson, Pitching Pioneer." NPR, *Morning Edition*, 18 February 2003.

Essington, A. "Alice Marie Coachman (1923–2014)." BlackPast.org, 2009, https://www.blackpast.org/african-american-history/coachman-alice-marie-1923 (accessed 8 March 2020).

Farley, Andrew. "Petition to Place Mamie Johnson into the Hall of Fame." MoveOn .org, 2018, https://sign.moveon.org/petitions/national-baseball-hall (accessed 16 September 2020).

First Tee of Northern California. "The First Tee Nor Cal Leadership Academy." first-teesacramento.org.

Flood, Curt. "Letter from Curt Flood to the Commissioner of Baseball, Bowie K. Kuhn, 1969." National Archives 278312.

Fontanez, Maria. "With All the Honors, Millito Is 100." *African American Sports Magazine*, June 2006.

Freedman, Lew. *Latino Baseball Legends: An Encyclopedia*. Westport, CT: Greenwood, 2010.

Gaetjens, Lesly. *The Shot Heard Around the World: The Joe Gaetjens Story*. Morrisville, NC: Lulu.com, 2010.

Gerard, Joseph. "Millito Navarro." Society for American Baseball Research, 2018, https://sabr.org/bioproj/person/millito-navarro (accessed 13 March 2022).

Gloster, Rob. "Pioneering Sports Journalist Sam Skinner Dead at 56." Associated Press News, 11 January 1996.

Goldstein, Richard. "Alice Coachman, 90, Dies: First Black Woman to Win Olympic Gold." *New York Times*, 14 July 2014.

Green, Jesse. "America's Pastime Meets America's Problem." *New York Times*, 20 June 2019.

Green, Michelle. *A Strong Right Arm: The Story of Mamie "Peanut" Johnson*. London: Puffin Books, 2004.

Greider, Katherine. "The Schoolteacher on the Streetcar." New York Times, 13 November 2005.

Harris, Doug. *Bounce: The Don Barksdale Story*. Documentary film. Doug Harris Media, 2016.

Hatch, Orrin, sponsor. "The Curt Flood Act of 1998." U.S. Congress, 1998, www .congress.gov (accessed 14 March 2020).

Henderson, Leah. *Mamie on the Mound: A Woman in Baseball's Negro Leagues*. Chicago: Capstone, 2020.

Hill, Urla. *Speed City Era: The Coaches*. San Jose State College "Speed City" Collection, 2007.

Hodak, George. "Track & Field: An Olympian's Oral History; Archie Williams 1936 Olympic Games." Amateur Athletic Foundation of Los Angeles, 15 June 1988.

Howard, Eli. "Funeral Services for Lieutenant Colonel Eli Page Howard." *Standard Star* (New Rochelle, NY), 29 August 1969.

Jackson, Scoop. "It's Time to Honor Spencer Haywood's Impact on Hoops and History." ESPN.com, 2015, https://www.espn.com/nba/story/_/id/13627349/ spencer-haywood-impact-hoops-history (accessed 10 September 2021).

Johnson, Janet. "Sistas on the Links Women's Golf Club." www.sistasonthelinks.net, established December 2011.

Kernan, Kevin. "Li'l Lady Dazzled Negro League Hit Men." *New York Post*, 3 June 2001.

Khatib, Arif. African American Ethnic Sports Hall of Fame Induction Ceremony. June 2005.

Khatib, Arif, and Steven Bernier. *Because They Believed*. Documentary film. Oakland, CA: HyperMedia Arts, Street Dreams Productions, 2021.

Kim, Tae Yun. "He Can Do, She Can Do, Why Not Me?" www.taeyunkim.com.

Kim, Tae Jun. *Seven Steps to Inner Power: How to Break through to Awesome*. Medford, OR: Mountain Tiger Press, 2018.

Kraetzer, Ken. "Memorial Day: Remembering Two Army Veterans from Morgan State." *Bleacher Report*, 29 May 2011.

Kukura, Joe. "Mission Bay Is Getting Five New Street Room Sculptures." *Hoodline*, 12 April 2022, hoodline.com/2022/04/mission-bay-is-getting-five-new-street-room-sculptures-including-one-by-former-kpix-anchor-dana-king.

Lacy, Sam. *Baltimore Afro-American*, 10 November 1945.

Lang, Arne. "At Age 80, Multifaceted Thell Torrence Is Still a Force in the Boxing Game." *The Sweet Science*, 13 October 2016.

Lang, Sarah. "The Negro Leagues Only Female Pitcher." MLB.com, *Slang on Sports*, 2018, https://www.mlb.com/history/negro-leagues/players/mamie-johnson (accessed 6 August 2021).

Langer, Emily. "Alice Coachman, First Black Woman to Win an Olympic Gold Medal, Dies at 91." *Washington Post*, 15 July 2014.

"A Life Well-Lived, the Story of Dr. Sammy Lee." www.thesammyleestory.com (accessed 16 April 2022).

Litsky, Frank. "Mal Whitfield, Olympic Gold Medalist and Tuskegee Airman, Dies at 91." *New York Times*, 19 November 2015.

Litsky, Frank. "Willye B. White, the First 5-Time U.S. Track Olympian, Dies at 67." *New York Times*, 7 February 2007.

Livingstone, Seth. "Former Negro Leaguer Millito Navarro Still Swinging the Bat at Age 104." *USA Today*, 28 July 2010.

Long Road to Justice. "The African American Experience in the Massachusetts Courts; Edward Gourdin." Massachusetts Historical Society, 2017, https://www.masshist.org (accessed 11 April 2021).

Lutz, John. "Manny McIntyre: Elite Athlete & Sports Pioneer." Virtual presentation for the Fredericton Region Museum, 7 February 2022.

"'Marvelous Mal' Whitfield." Whitfield Foundation, 2004, http://www.whitfield-foundation.org/about/index2.html (accessed 5 May 2022).

McAllister, Mike. "Breakthrough at Burneyville." PGAtour.com, 2014, https://www .pgatour.com/news/2014/04/29/pete-brown-first-win-african-american.html (accessed 29 April 2022).

Meyer, Eugene. "A True American Athlete." *Washington Post*, 3 February 1999.

Mills, Billy. *Wokini: A Lakota Journey to Happiness and Self-Understanding.* Quincy, CA: Feather Publishing, 1990.

Monagan, Matt. "The Youngest Ballplayer Ever Was HOW Old?" MLB.com, 2021, https://www.mlb.com/news/youngest-player-in-baseball-history (accessed 12 February 2022).

Morgan State Hall of Fame. "Eddie Hurt." 2021. https://morganstatebears.com/ honors/hall-of-fame/edward-hurt/23 (accessed 6 March 2022).

Morris, Gabrielle. "The Joy of Flying: Olympic Gold, Air Force Colonel, and Teacher, Archie F. Williams." University of California Black Alumni Series, 11 February 1992.

Moye, Todd. Freedom Flyers: The Tuskegee Airmen of World War II (New York: Oxford University Press, 2012.

Musil, Steven. "Google Doodle Honors Toni Stone, Trailblazing Female Pro Baseball Player." CNET.com, 2022, https://www.cnet.com/culture 2022 (accessed 8 April 2022).

Obera, Irene. "Faces in the Crowd." SI Vault, 18 June 1962.

Obera, Irene. "Faces in the Crowd." SI Vault, 13 June 2014.

Obera, Irene. "Faces in the Crowd." SI Vault, 18 January 2019.

Raymond, Ken. "Oklahoma's Crown Jewel." *Oklahoma Eagle*, 7 June 2017.

Reagan, Ronald. "About Mal Whitfield." Whitfield Foundation, 2004, http://www .whitfieldfoundation.org (accessed 16 November 2020).

Rhoden, William. "Sports of the Times; Good Things Happening for One Who Decided to Wait." *New York Times*, 27 April 1995.

Rollow, Cooper. "Cardinals: 1958 Season May Determine Cards' Future in the Windy City." In *1958 Pro Football.* Los Angeles, CA: Petersen, 1958.

San Francisco Police Department. "Award Ceremony Honoring Burl Toler." 2009.

Schudel, Matt. "Mamie 'Peanut' Johnson, Hard-Throwing Woman in Baseball's Negro Leagues, Dies at 82." *Washington Post*, 21 December 2017.

Schulz, Mark. "Burl Toler Blazed a Trail 50 Years Ago." *Profiles, Football Zebras*, 2016, www.footballzebras.com (accessed 7 February 2021).

Shapiro, Donald. "Chi Cheng Taking Physical Therapy." *New York Times*, 30 April 1972.

Staff. "Emilio 'Millito' Navarro Dies at 105." Associated Press, 1 May, 2011.

Staff. "For the Record." *Sports Illustrated*, 12 July 1965.

Staff. "Harvard-Yale Overwhelms English Rivals." *Boston Post*, 24 July 1921.

Staff. *New York Telegram*, 24 July 1921.

Stafford, Chris. "Irene Obera, American Sprinter." WISP conversations from the world of women's sports interview, 2016, https://www.wispsports.com/the-bolder-woman/s2e2/irene-obera-american-sprinter (accessed 16 September, 2019).

Stone, Ken. "Hall of Famer Irene Obera Comes Out of Retirement, Claims W80 WR." Masterstrack.com, 2018, http://masterstrack.com/hall-of-famer-irene-obera-comes-out-of-retirement-claims-w80-wr (accessed June 2021).

Tatum, Bill. "Edward Orval Gourdin." 2010. www.eogourdin.com (accessed 7 January 2020).

Taylor, Erica. "Little Known Black History Fact: Boley, Oklahoma." *Tom Joyner Morning Show*, 30 October 2012, www. blackamericaweb.com.

Taylor, Marshall. *The Fastest Bicycle Rider in the World: The Story of a Colored Boy's Indomitable Courage and Success against Great Odds*. Stratford, NH: Ayer Company, 1928.

"The USF 1951 Dons: The Team That Stood Tall." NFL.com, 27 January 2016.

"Top 100 Greatest NFL Players of All Time." *Sporting News* (Charlotte, NC), 1 November 1999.

Trone, David (D-MD). "Letter for Curt Flood's Nomination and Induction into the Baseball Hall of Fame." Sent to the Baseball Hall of Fame, 2017, https://trone.house.gov/2021/06/28/letter-for-curt-floods-nomination-and-induction-into-the-baseball-hall-of-fame (accessed 28 June 2021).

Truman, Harry. Executive Order 9981 Ending Segregation in the Armed Forces. National Archives Foundation, 26 July 1948.

"U.S. Forces Blocked from Downed Copter." U.S. Army Archives, 2015, http://www.arlingtoncemetery.net (accessed 15 July 2021).

Van Leuven, Holly. "For a Black Man, the Negro Leagues Could Be a Trial of Resilience. Imagine Being a Woman." *Sports Illustrated*, 13 October 2020.

Vrabel, Jim. *When in Boston: A Time Line & Almanac*. Lebanon, NH: Northeastern University Press, 2004.

Wade, Herman. *Run from There: A Biography of Edward P. Hurt*. Tarentum, PA: Word Association Publishers, 2003.

Walker, Rhiannon. "The Day Alice Coachman Became the First Black Woman to Win Olympic Gold." 8 August 2018. www.andscape.com.

Washington University. "Interview with Alice Coachman." *Black Champion Series*, 1985, http://repository.wustl.edu (accessed 3 April 2022).

Weber, Bruce. "Burl Toler, First Black N.F.L. Official, Dies at 81." *New York Times*, 20 August 2009.

"Why Two Black Athletes Raised Their Fists during the Anthem." *New York Times*, 16 October, 2018.

Williams, Eric. "The Greatest Black Female Athletes of All Time." BlackAthlete.net, 6 April 2006.

Williams, Ted. "Induction Speech." National Baseball Hall of Fame, Cooperstown, NY, 1966, https://www.mlb.com/news/ted-williams-hall-of-fame-speech-honored-negro-league-players (accessed 15 August 2020).

Wilson, Nick. *Early Latino Players in the United States: Major, Minor and Negro Leagues*. Jefferson, NC: McFarland, 2005.

Witt, Richard. *A Lifetime of Training for Just Ten Seconds: Olympians in Their Own Words*. London: A and C Black, 2012.

Woo, Elaine. "Mal Whitfield Dies at 91; Runner Won Two Olympic Golds in 800-Meter Event." *LA Times*, 20 November 2015.

Woodruff, John. "Paying Tribute to Long John's L-O-N-G Gold-Medal Run." *Pitt Chronicle*, 11 September 2006.

Yoo, Paula. *Sixteen Years in Sixteen Seconds: The Sammy Lee Story*. New York: Lee & Low Books, 2005.

Index

Page references for figures are italicized.

About the Authors

Arif Khatib is originally from Arkansas. As a child, he moved to Richmond, California. Khatib would go on to establish several companies, among them a record label, a publishing company, an entertainment production company, and a boxing promotion company. As an instructor of labor management at the University of California, Berkeley, he helped develop and implement minority and women's businesses and participated in affirmation action, youth crime, drug abuse, and incarceration seminars. In 2000, Khatib created the African American Ethnic Sports Hall of Fame. He has been a consultant to athletes and entertainers. In 2021, he produced the documentary film *Because They Believed*. Previous works include *Re-establishing and Maintaining Good Credit*, *A Women's Ticket to Understanding Football*, *Real Estate Creative Financing*, the *African American Sports Magazine*, and *Scoop the News*.

Pete Elman is a musician, journalist, author, and teacher. He is originally from Washington, DC, where his father, a civil rights lawyer who argued before the Supreme Court, imbued in him a sense of social justice. In 1973, he moved to California, and since that time he has worked as a nationally known performer, composer, studio musician, recording artist, and producer.

Elman worked for the Bay Area News Group covering prep and college sports from 2000 to 2011. From 2000 to

2005, he was the resident columnist for the *Oakland Athletics Fan Coalition*, and he currently contributes to the *Ultimate Sports Guide*. In 2013, he released an acclaimed children's picture book, *Seasons, Rhymes in Time*. He has taught public school and is currently teaching adult courses on popular American music and sports at several Bay Area universities.